The Dissertation Journey

Fourth Edition

The Dissertation Journey

A Practical and Comprehensive Guide to Planning, Writing, and Defending Your Dissertation

Fourth Edition

Laura Hyatt | Carol Roberts

FOR INFORMATION:

Corwin

A SAGE Company

2455 Teller Road

Thousand Oaks, California 91320

(800) 233-9936

www.corwin.com

SAGE Publications Ltd.

1 Oliver's Yard

55 City Road

London EC1Y 1SP

United Kingdom

SAGE Publications India Pvt. Ltd.

Unit No 323-333, Third Floor, F-Block

International Trade Tower Nehru Place

New Delhi 110 019

India

SAGE Publications Asia-Pacific Pte. Ltd.

18 Cross Street #10-10/11/12

China Square Central

Singapore 048423

Vice President and
   Editorial Director: Monica Eckman

Program Director and Publisher: Dan Alpert

Content Development Manager: Lucas Schleicher

Content Development Editor: Mia Rodriguez

Editorial Assistant: Natalie Delpino

Project Editor: Amy Schroller

Copy Editor: Erin Livingston

Typesetter: C&M Digitals (P) Ltd.

Cover Designer: Gail Buschman

Marketing Manager: Melissa Duclos

Printed in Canada

Library of Congress Cataloging-in-Publication Data

Names: Hyatt, Laura, author. | Roberts, Carol, author.

Title: The dissertation journey : a practical and comprehensive guide to planning, writing, and defending your dissertation / Laura Hyatt, Carol Roberts.

Description: Fourth edition. | Thousand Oaks, California: Corwin, 2024. | Includes bibliographical references and index.

Identifiers: LCCN 2023015714 | ISBN 9781071891285 (paperback) | ISBN 9781071891292 (epub) | ISBN 9781071891308 (epub) | ISBN 9781071891315 (pdf)

Classification: LCC LB1742 .R63 2024 | DDC 808/.066378—dc23/eng/20230522

LC record available at https://lccn.loc.gov/2023015714

This book is printed on acid-free paper.

23 24 25 26 27 10 9 8 7 6 5 4 3 2 1

Contents

New to This Edition

We appreciate the opportunity to write a fourth edition of *The Dissertation Journey: A Practical and Comprehensive Guide to Planning, Writing, and Defending Your Dissertation.* The fourth edition includes new information as well as updates of previous topics that we hope will help you successfully navigate the dissertation process.

The fourth edition has been reviewed and revised to offer the reader current information. The revisions provided an opportunity to restructure, amalgamate, and redistribute the material throughout the book. This resulted in greater efficacy and clarity.

The resources sections incorporated at the end of the chapters are also updated and revised. The resources include websites that are useful throughout the course of completing the dissertation. Additionally, there is a new section in Chapter 15 titled "Mountain Echos" that offers the reader an opportunity to hear from recent doctoral candidates who have been successful in the journey.

Preface

The Dissertation Journey offers both scholarly and practical guidance about planning, writing, and defending a dissertation. Doctoral students will (1) understand it as a research study as well as a psychological and human relations venture; (2) get a clear picture of what it takes to write a high-quality research study and see it as doable; (3) feel encouraged and supported in their efforts; (4) experience the process as a satisfying, rewarding, and exciting journey; and (5) finish!

It is important to note that while this book contains elements of theory, research, and methods, it is not intended to replace a theoretical research methodology book. We wrote this book to satisfy the existing need for a clear and concise guidebook focused on significant processes for completing a doctoral dissertation. *The Dissertation Journey* provides guidance on how to plan, write, and defend a dissertation. Its structure parallels the dissertation progression and presents detailed information about the content and process from conceptualizing a topic to publishing the results. It addresses the emotional barriers students confront and provides up-to-date online resources for the various stages of dissertating. The style is personal and conversational—much like a coach talking one-on-one with a student. To enhance learning and clarify concepts, we included a myriad of examples together with helpful hints, resources, checklists, and quotations. Since writing a dissertation can be a bewildering and overwhelming experience for students, we use the metaphor of climbing a mountain for inspiration and for motivation to persevere in spite of obstacles.

The techniques, insights, and knowledge we gained from years of experience teaching and guiding dissertation students serve as a valuable road map for the dissertation journey and, hopefully, make the task more understandable, more manageable, and less time-consuming. This is not intended to be a complete work on writing dissertations, nor could it be; the scope would be overwhelming. The book does not include detailed information on certain aspects of academic research, such as design and methodology, data analysis techniques, or writing style and mechanics.

This book is geared toward the specific needs and concerns of doctoral students as they proceed through each step of the dissertation process. It focuses primarily on the social sciences; however, graduate students in most academic disciplines desiring to complete a research study will find the book's content useful and applicable. Generally, the steps for writing a dissertation or thesis are much the same, regardless of the topic or discipline; they vary primarily in scope and complexity. Graduate faculty involved with student research will also find the book's ideas and suggestions beneficial. Universities vary considerably in their dissertation requirements and procedures. In addition, there is considerable diversity among the preferences of advisors and departments within a university. Students should consult their dissertation advisor, as they are responsible for guiding this process. The suggestions offered in this book, therefore, should not be considered final nor should they preempt the judgment and opinions of dissertation advisors, chairs, and committees.

Researching and writing a dissertation or thesis should be a rewarding experience—one students can comprehend and (most of all) complete. It is our hope that this book, with its straight talk, step-by-step guidance, and practical advice will make the journey to "doctor" smoother and, in the process, help students reach their goals and successfully complete their dissertation.

Note to
Doctoral Students

Congratulations for taking the steps to embark on a new and exciting journey—obtaining a doctoral degree. This journey generally requires completing a dissertation, the pinnacle of academic achievement. In many ways, the journey is similar to climbing a high mountain; it is a long and arduous trek—not for the fainthearted. It offers incomparable opportunities for personal and professional growth.

Reaching the summit of a mountain symbolizes the process you go through to complete your dissertation. The climb tests your mettle and challenges your resolve, but once you complete it and experience the magnificent view from the top, you realize the rewards far outweigh the effort. The exhilaration and pride of accomplishment, the fulfillment that results from contribution, a deeper self-awareness, and greater confidence in yourself as a scholar are only a few of the rewards that await you.

It may be that you see your own dissertation as a looming mountain—massive and awesome—with the accompanying feelings of doubt and apprehension. However, you will learn that journeying to the peak is more than an intellectual pilgrimage; it is also an emotional one. It requires commitment, perseverance, stamina, and mental toughness—more than you ever thought you had.

Completing a dissertation changes your life. You will discover that your primary reward was not so much the exhilaration of standing on top of the mountain at the journey's end but rather who you became as a result of the climb. Only by taking yourself to the limit can you know what you're made of. Sir Edmund Hillary, one of the first men to reach the summit of Mount Everest, said "It is not the mountain we conquer, but ourselves."

We wrote this book to help make your journey to the summit a satis-fying and rewarding one. In these pages, we speak to you informally as an advisor and colleague about the entire dissertation process. Plus, we speak about those critical issues related to the personal and social side of dissertating (organization, time management, human relations, etc.).

The material presented in this book represents years spent guiding dis-sertation students and researching the literature on this topic. Please remember that the ideas and recommendations provided should be used only as a guide. Your advisor and committee are the ultimate sources of information and instruction about your dissertation.

Source: https//iStock.com/mstipek

It is our hope that you catch summit fever and become motivated to reach the top. Do bring a spirit of adventure to this journey and, by all means, enjoy the climb! We wish you happy writing with the warm-est regards!

Acknowledgments

We didn't climb this high mountain alone. Experience, expertise, support, and encouragement were all needed. We are grateful to those who provided these necessities, which helped make this book a reality.

We want to thank those doctoral students we have had the privilege of working with—and particularly those who invited us to chair their dissertations. They continue to help us understand the unique challenges associated with doctoral students conducting high-quality dissertation research.

We were fortunate to work with a talented editorial publishing team from Corwin. We want to express our appreciation for Dan Alpert, program director and publisher, who was patient and always there to respond to our questions about developing, writing, and revising the manuscript. We also want to thank Lucas Schleicher, content development manager, and all the people at Corwin who helped make this book a reality.

In addition, we want to recognize the reviewers and the team who edited the book. We appreciate your time, efforts, patience, and valuable input.

We want to thank Stephanie Voss, doctoral candidate and Ryan Gordy, doctoral student who provided valuable assistance in researching and updating online sources.

We appreciate the new doctors and doctoral candidates who offered their wisdom in the new "Mountain Echos" section.

Laura is grateful to her family and friends, especially Dave and Molly, who encouraged her writing, challenged her to try new things, and provided unconditional love. She also appreciates all the teachers, mentors, and colleagues along the way who sparked her curiosity and fueled her imagination. Laura is thankful for the opportunity to collaborate on this book with Carol. Our similar writing styles and work ethic, combined with our friendship and respect for one another, contributed to the successful completion of this project.

Carol deeply appreciates the ongoing love of her husband, Edward, whose patience and support inspired confidence to leave "base camp" for the many physical and academic climbs that resulted in an adventurous and fulfilled life. Carol is also grateful to her coauthor, Laura, a friend and colleague whose research expertise provided invaluable insights into the content and process of completing a high-quality dissertation for this book.

About the Authors

Laura Hyatt is a professor and chair at Pepperdine University, Graduate School of Education and Psychology—Education Division. She is also the executive director of academic affairs for the Graduate School of Education Division where she encourages scholarly research. She is an associate of a global think tank, participated as an advisor to the office of the assistant secretary for planning and evaluation at the Department of Health and Human Services in Washington, DC, and was appointed to a White House policy conference by the president of the United States. Previously, Dr. Hyatt was a tenured professor and chair at the University of La Verne where she earned emeritus status. Prior to teaching, she was vice president of education for a production company and part of a collaborative effort that won several awards in the entertainment industry. She earned her doctorate degree from Pepperdine University. Dr. Hyatt has authored books, book chapters, and journal articles and serves on editorial boards for peer-reviewed journals. Dr. Hyatt has received recognition and grants for her research which focuses on the intersections of learning, neuroscience, change, and the powerful climates created by our convergent stories as individuals, organizations, and communities.

Carol Roberts is a professor emerita from the University of La Verne where she taught leadership in the doctoral program. She advised doctoral students, chaired dissertations, and taught a variety of leadership courses primarily in personal leadership, communication, conflict, and coaching. She has served as a consultant and seminar leader specializing in organizational and team development, strategic planning, conflict resolution, coaching, and personal mastery. Dr. Roberts has been a consultant and trainer for the administrator trainer center and effective schools program, the California School Leadership Academy, and the California School Boards Association. She received her doctoral degree in planning, policy, and administration from the University of Southern California. Carol has also served on the executive board for the Southern Counties Women in Educational Management and was awarded its Woman of the Year award.

PART I

Preparing for the Journey

Source: https://istockphoto.com/hadynyah

The journey of a thousand miles begins and ends with one step.

—Lao Tse

Personal Considerations 1

Throughout the ages, people pursued the upper limits of their capabilities. They answered the call to adventure, learning, and high achievement. Completing the dissertation journey is an adventure in learning and personal growth, the outcome of which can result in extraordinary accomplishment and contribution. Unquestionably, obtaining a doctorate degree (e.g., EdD, PhD, DBA, etc.) is the summit of academia—the highest degree any university can bestow. This journey to "doctor" is difficult with obstacles and demands along the way; however, once completed, the pride and exultation are a lifelong affirmation.

A doctorate usually requires completion of a dissertation that demonstrates your ability to plan, conduct, write, and defend an original research study. In many ways, the dissertation process is a journey not unlike climbing a difficult mountain. The journey is arduous and long, usually three to five years from beginning to end, and it is easy to become frustrated, exhausted, and discouraged. It is grueling—definitely not for anyone who lacks commitment or perseverance. Those who successfully scale the peak are those willing to put in long hours and hard work.

Writing a dissertation is a personal transformative experience and can be a peak experience—one of those life-fulfilling moments. Maslow (1968) referred to them as "moments of highest happiness and fulfillment" (p. 73) and added, "A peak experience is felt as a self-validating, self-justifying moment which carries its own intrinsic value with it" (p. 79). He claimed that the worth of the experience makes the pain worthwhile. Schuller (1980) also talked about peak experiences in

> People do not decide to become extraordinary. They decide to accomplish extraordinary things.
>
> —Edmund Hillary

his book, *The Peak to Peek Principle.* He called a peak experience "an experience of success, achievement, and accomplishment which feeds your self-esteem, which then expands your self-confidence" (p. 99) and added, "It's an experience that leaves you with an awareness that you are more than you ever thought you were" (p. 113).

These positive, uplifting, and inspiring words speak to the high accomplishment of completing a doctoral dissertation. Many high points and joys happen along the dissertation journey—some simple, some exhilarating. Moments such as realizing you really do have a researchable topic, having your proposal accepted, obtaining an acceptable questionnaire return rate, and creative moments and intellectual insights are all triumphs along the path. The instant your advisor calls you "doctor," the ecstasy of walking to "Pomp and Circumstance" at graduation, and when your doctoral hood is placed over your head are self-fulfilling, unforgettable moments that make the hard work and sacrifice worthwhile.

Research has revealed that the attitude you have at the beginning of a task determines the outcome of that task more than any other single factor. For example, if you believe you will be able to succeed at a particular undertaking and you approach the endeavor with a sense of excitement and joyful expectation, your chances of achieving success are much higher than if you face the task with dread and apprehension.

—Abascal et al. (2001, p. 39)

Unfortunately, there is a mythology that supports a negative view that completing a dissertation is demeaning and full of drudgery, consisting only of a series of hoops to jump through and hurdles to overcome. Students who adopt this mindset spend much of their time whining and "awfulizing" their experiences. They bemoan their plight and feel tormented throughout the entire process. It is a truism that completing a dissertation is hard work, time-consuming, frustrating, and, at times, frightening—this is a given. It takes a good deal of self-discipline and courage to undertake a project of this magnitude.

What makes the difference between a peak experience and a heartbreak hill experience? Attitude. Attitude is everything! On the mountain and in life, our attitude makes or breaks us. If you think you can do it, then you can.

Approaching the dissertation journey with a spirit of adventure, optimism, and a can-do attitude helps ensure that you will succeed and achieve a peak experience in the process. Climbing a mountain peak is a powerful metaphor; it represents the path to growth and transformation. The obstacles encountered along the way embody the challenges that help expand your thinking and your boundaries. The risks are substantial, the sacrifices great. However, the view is magnificent from the top, and it is reserved for those courageous adventurers who dare to challenge their own limits. Ultimately, though, it's the journey itself that results in self-validative delight, not merely standing at the top. Once you are there, you will not be the same person or ever again look at the world in the same light.

With hard work and perseverance, we will see you at the top.

> The primary reward is not the goal but what you become as a result of doing all that was necessary to reach the goal.
>
> —David McNalley

Do You Have What It Takes to Journey to the Peak?

Remember the travelers on the yellow brick road? They wanted to get to the Emerald City, yet each had to be transformed in order to get there. They needed three things to find their way: brains, heart, and courage. You will need the merging of these same three things to successfully complete your dissertation journey. Cognitive ability is necessary but not sufficient. Certainly, you must put all your intellectual powers to work in conducting your study and analyzing its results. Such powers do make for easier climbing. However, it's your heart—the spirit and passion you bring—that sustains you for the long haul. The third critical need is courage—the ability to dig deep into yourself and persevere when the going gets tough and you want to quit. You will find that when you think you cannot go another step, there is an untapped and astonishing reservoir of sustenance that can pull you through—mind over matter.

Forward thinking the following can help you better understand what it takes to climb the dissertation mountain—that final challenge to obtaining your doctorate. Just remember that you can, and probably will, accomplish more under sometimes-adverse conditions than you may believe.

Considerations for the Challenges Ahead

There is no true success in any large-scale endeavor without sacrifice. Self-discipline is the name of the game. Are you willing to give up momentary pleasures for your long-term goal? To burn some midnight oil? Completing the dissertation is a demanding task and takes time, money, and energy which can affect all aspects of your life. It can cause strained relationships with your spouse, partner, children, friends, and work colleagues. It can affect your work assignment, causing conflicts between time spent doing your dissertation and time spent doing your job. Be realistic about the financial costs connected with conducting a research study, such as typing, copying, library expenses, consultants, travel, postage, telephone calls, computer costs, and so on.

The path is fraught with difficulties and obstacles. Can you face them without becoming discouraged? Are you prepared for the stress that accompanies emotional setbacks and extra demands on your time? The dissertation process is often obscure and perplexing, requiring a high level of tolerance for ambiguity and uncertainty. It means often working outside your comfort zone. Are you willing to risk the unknown and to be teachable? If not, you can wander around aimlessly in the foothills of confusion and frustration. Are you willing to learn as you go?

> That which we obtain too easily, we esteem too lightly.
>
> —Thomas Paine

It is important to recognize the downsides, the consequences, and the risks of taking the dissertation journey. If you believe that you have what it takes, you can climb the mountain, stand on the top, and feel the joy of high achievement.

Avoiding the Dissertation Hazards Along the Path

Climbing real or metaphoric mountains can be hazardous to your health. It can sap your energy and weaken your resolve to endure to the top. Just as mountaineers must be mindful of potential avalanches, crevasses, high winds, falling rocks, and storms, researchers, too, must be aware of the dissertation hazards along their path. These hazards can hinder your progress in completing your dissertation.

Dissertating is not only an intellectual endeavor but also a psychological one to which most graduates will attest. It is truly a personal pilgrimage—one that tests your stamina, self-confidence, and emotional resilience. The only way you will ever become a doctor is to willingly struggle against the obstacles that get in your way and to do so without quitting. Be forewarned. You will want to quit, but *quitting* and *wanting to quit* are very different things. The inner resources you bring to the task keep you on the path. These inner resources are discussed later in this chapter.

Being aware of the hazards of dissertating helps you select suitable routes and make adjustments to overcome the risks. Make no mistake, dissertating is high-altitude climbing! Four hazards of this high-altitude climbing that you should be aware of are procrastination, emotional barriers, writer's block, and lack of concentration. The next sections describe these hazards and provide some strategies for dealing with them.

Procrastination

To *procrastinate* means to intentionally and habitually put off doing something that should be done. It is a habit that steals away some of life's greatest opportunities, yet it is a habit most of us possess. Many books deal with overcoming procrastination, yet we seem to either put off reading them or fail to heed their advice. This habit, quite common among dissertation students, can result in an ABD (all-but-dissertation) status rather than an EdD, DBA, or PhD. This amounts to aborting the climb to the peak and settling for heartbreak hill. We are acutely aware of the whole complex of dazzling excuses proffered by dissertation writers. With some doctoral students, we've found that dissertation avoidance is often elevated to an elegant art form. Certainly, there are occasionally excellent reasons for putting off working on your dissertation. Emergencies, interruptions from others, and acts of God happen to all of us from time to time. However, the students we worry about are those who keep themselves from starting or continuing because they fear the unknown, lack the self-confidence to move ahead on their own, or engage in irrational thinking, such as "awfulizing." They convince themselves the task is awful, horrible, and unbearable. But putting it off only postpones the inevitable. It is critical that you learn to recognize those signs that indicate you are putting off working.

> Putting off an easy thing makes it hard, and putting off a hard one makes it impossible.
>
> —George H. Lorimer

There are two physical laws that apply equally well to people and objects with regard to the habit of procrastination. They are Newton's law of inertia and Parkinson's law.

The Law of Inertia

The law of inertia states the following: A body in motion tends to stay in motion; a body at rest tends to stay at rest. In other words, it takes greater force to get a body moving than it does to keep it moving, and when it gets moving, it takes less force to keep it moving than to stop it. Physical inertia is regulated by outside forces, but the real changes in our life's attitudes and habits come from within. As William James said,

"The greatest discovery of my generation is that a person can alter his life by altering his attitude of mind." Those who succeed do so because when they head toward a specific destination, they keep going until they reach it. It's hard to stop them.

People who procrastinate find many excuses for not moving up the mountain. Certainly, some excuses are quite legitimate—a family or health crisis and so on. But you cannot be productive if you allow yourself to procrastinate for long periods of time. To overcome inertia, you must get started and build momentum. Decide to do it now. Once you realize that inertia is a normal part of our human experience, it is easier to deal with.

A habit develops when you take action so many times that it becomes automatic. How does one break the procrastination habit? We found that the best way is to develop the reverse habit—refuse to procrastinate. If you refuse to procrastinate often enough, then that also becomes a habitual response.

Parkinson's Law

Parkinson's law is a ready-made excuse. It states, "Work expands to fill the time available for its completion." This law applies especially to dissertation writers. Many doctoral students have families and hold full-time jobs. It is so easy for other work (job and family obligations) to fill all the available time, leaving no time to write the dissertation. Competing demands for your time are always problematic, and let's face it, immediate gratification and family fun are more seductive than confronting your dissertation mountain.

So how do you overcome Parkinson's law? Invoke the Premack principle. The Premack principle, often called *grandma's rule*, states that a high-frequency activity can be used to reinforce low-frequency behavior. Access to the preferred activity is contingent on completing the low-frequency behavior. Grandma knew this simply as, "Before you can watch TV, you have to help with the dishes." This is a simple behavioral principle behind the "work first, play second" maxim. What is it you most like to do? Surf the internet? Watch TV? Shop? Complete a dissertation task, then do something you really enjoy; for example, "Before I can watch TV, I have to revise my questionnaire" or "If I complete Chapter 1, I can see a movie on the weekend." Disciplining yourself in this way keeps you on task and keeps your momentum in high gear. You will complete your dissertation in record time.

Here are some strategies to help reverse the habit of procrastination.

> Dreams are what get you started. Discipline is what keeps you going.
>
> —Jim Ryun

1. Challenge Your Excuses

Through the years, we've witnessed a variety of creative excuses offered by doctoral students to themselves and to their advisor. If you don't challenge the excuses you use, you may remain in stationary inertia, unable to make the forward progress you desire. One common excuse is "I haven't read enough to write yet." Argue with yourself that writing helps clarify your thinking, and, besides, first drafts don't have to be perfect. First drafts are first drafts; they are always improved by reviewing and rewriting. If one of your excuses is that you need deadlines to work effectively, argue with yourself that waiting until the deadline to get started results in undue stress and leaves you tired, uncreative, and irritable. It can also affect the quality of your writing. Conducting inner debates about any "logical" excuse keeps you from stalling. Following is a practice exercise developed by Hibbs (2004) to better understand and manage your excuses. He suggests that you write out every excuse you make for not working on your dissertation, then write a rebuttal for each excuse. He gives the following examples:

> The best way to break a habit is to drop it.
>
> —Leo Aikman

Excuse:	"I don't have the time."
Rebuttal:	"Maybe I only have a few minutes right now. Nevertheless, I can at least get started and get a few things finished."
Excuse:	"I just don't feel like doing it now."
Rebuttal:	"Maybe I don't feel like doing it. Nevertheless, I'll feel great once I get started and get something accomplished."
Excuse:	"I'm too tired. I don't have the energy."
Rebuttal:	"If someone gave me a million dollars to do this, I'd jump in with great enthusiasm. Energy is simply a matter of attitude. If I change my attitude, I'll have all the energy I need."
Excuse:	"It's too hard."
Rebuttal:	"Yes, it takes considerable effort. Nevertheless, if I keep at it, I can accomplish my goals."

The best way to achieve what you want is to have the courage to deny yourself any excuses! (p. 53)

Source: Hibbs (2004).

2. Develop a *Do It Now!* Habit

This self-motivator was recommended by Stone (1962) in *The Success System That Never Fails.* He claimed it sparks you to action. Here's what you do: Repeat "Do it now!" to yourself 50 times or more in the morning and evening and whenever it occurs to you throughout the day. This imprints it indelibly in your subconscious. Every time you must do something you don't feel like doing and the self-starter *Do it now!* flashes in your mind, immediately *act* (p. 93).

The *Do it now!* habit also helps when you're in the dissertation gloom-and-doom state. Consider adopting Waitley's (1987) personal motto, "Stop stewing and start doing." He said, "I can't be depressed and active at the same time" (p. 147).

Another technique to acquire this self-starting habit is to post a sign that says *Do it now!* around your house and desk. It helps jog your memory.

> Nothing is so fatiguing as the eternal hanging on of an uncompleted task.
>
> —William James

3. Divide and Conquer

Mountains are overwhelming and, in their entirety, intimidating. They can't be conquered all at once. In technical climbs, we move up the mountain in a series of pitches—one handhold and toehold at a time until we stand, spent but elated, on the top. Looking at the entire dissertation can also be overwhelming. Think of your dissertation as a mountain with stairs—a set of small steps leading to the top. It is important to break your dissertation down into small, achievable goals and take it step by step.

One strategy is to make a contract with yourself that states specific goals, establishes completion dates, and offers rewards for attaining your goals. It is important that you write these completion dates on your appointment calendar. There's a wonderful feeling of exhilaration that goes along with accomplishment. It gives you a new burst of energy to keep moving.

4. Remove the Reward

Procrastination should not be a pleasant experience. If you procrastinate by socializing or getting a cup of coffee, stop it! Procrastinate in unpleasant conditions. For example, lock yourself in your office—no visitors, no coffee. When the enjoyment goes away, so will your procrastination.

5. Discipline Yourself

If you really don't want to write, promise yourself you'll write for 15 minutes. Set a timer, and when it rings, decide if you will work for

15 more minutes or quit. Often, the hardest part is starting. This strategy helps you build that momentum to overcome inertia.

Emotional Barriers

Students often describe their experience of writing the dissertation as a roller-coaster ride, with definite ups and downs associated with each phase of the process. They refer to the down times as the *dissertation doldrums* where they feel discouraged, depressed, frustrated, and anxious. They even doubt their ability to complete the project. These feelings are predictable for anyone trying to achieve a high goal; however, these negative emotions can easily overpower you. If you don't address them, they will immobilize you, sap your energy, and keep you from achieving your goal. When things go well, you are elated and you soar on cloud nine. These feelings of exhilaration provide the momentum to "keep on keeping on." The ups and downs of dissertating—the pains and the joys—are experienced by all writers. It's part of the dissertation process and to be expected. The following are some strategies to help you deal with the dissertation doldrums.

1. Reflect on Your Reasons for Obtaining Your Doctorate

Sometimes you question your own sanity for undertaking this massive project. You wonder why you continue to torture yourself in this way. When you have these feelings, take time to reflect on the reasons you decided to enroll in a doctoral program. More than likely, they are still valid and should serve to reinforce your commitment and motivation to stay on track. Take time to reflect on these reasons, write them down, and visualize your life after graduation and a title after your name.

2. Establish a Support Committee

When the going gets rough, you may reach an impasse in your progress. That's when you assemble a support committee of friends, mentors, and family members—those who believe in you and have your best interests at heart. You might ask your mother to chair this committee. These are your cheerleaders and confidants when you're down; they share your joys and bad days and provide regular pep talks to overcome your discouragement. They also let you know when you are indulging yourself in complaining and offer you encouragement rather than pampering.

Writer's Block

All dissertation writers experience writer's block at some point during the process. It's that longing to be anywhere but in front of the computer. When this happens, everything else in your life takes priority over writing. Taking the dog for a walk, cleaning your closets, running errands, washing clothes, and emailing friends appear crucial. Writer's block can be caused by any number of factors: lack of confidence, fear, time constraints, no outline, personal issues, frustration with your topic, perfectionism, weariness. It is important to identify the obstacles that stifle your writing. In other words, take time to fall back and regroup. Unfortunately, there is no magic formula to keep you in the writing groove, but here are some strategies that might help you keep the words flowing.

1. Change the Mode of Putting Down Words

If you're stuck on the computer, try a dictation machine or writing by hand or change where you write—go outside, to a friendly coffee shop, or to the library.

2. Get Some Physical Exercise

Get outside and walk or mow the lawn. Physical activity of the pleasant and slightly mindless kind can precipitate creative thinking.

3. Make Two Lists

This exercise helps you get a handle on the root of your block. Whenever you are trying to write your dissertation but find yourself blank-minded and wordless, write two lists labeled as follows:

1. I ought to write X because . . .

2. I refuse to write X because . . .

The second list will be more informative than the first in that it brings to your conscious mind the refusals that may be lying at the subconscious level. You can then take steps to overcome your refusals.

4. Cluster Your Ideas

This is the old psychology game where one person says a word and the second person responds immediately with the very next word that comes to mind. First, write your subject on paper and circle it. Then, write down the very next thing you think of and circle that. Draw a line connecting these two circles. Next, write down what you thought of as you wrote the second word and draw a line connecting it to the previous word. Follow this process until you have exhausted your brain!

Write down everything that comes to your mind no matter how far out. After you complete the entire process, you will be amazed at the words that popped out.

A similar method that works for students is to cluster ideas using sticky notes. In the center of a large poster-size paper, write your subject and surround it with large circles. Then write all ideas connected with the subject on sticky notes and place them inside the circles. If desired, you can then use extra-small colored tags to add ideas to the larger notes. The beauty of this method is that you can move the sticky notes around as necessary. This mind-storming technique works well with collaborative groups. It allows individuals to build on ideas generated by others, thereby obtaining a broader perspective on the subject.

5. Write a Crummy First Draft

Perfectionists cringe at this thought. Just know that no one, however gifted, can write an acceptable first draft.

You don't have to write something *good* initially. Thinking that you do only causes self-disparagement and self-recrimination. Remember, first drafts are only *first* drafts and are for your eyes only. Let them be sketchy thoughts, rambling sentences, clumsy word patterns using poor grammar, and so on. Just get everything out of your brain and onto paper. Don't obsess and ponder ideas too long. Don't judge it, just *write it*. Getting your ideas on paper gets you moving. You now have something to work on and revise. Accept the fact that you will be writing several drafts, and take the pressure off the first one by concentrating only on your ideas. Most writers agree that it's easier to revise than to create. Writing is a complex and slow process, so don't expect it to flow effortlessly. Few writers write only when they feel inspired. If you wait for inspiration or write only when you feel like it, your chances of completion are nil.

Although all of the preceding suggestions are useful, over time, you will work out your own best ways and means for moving on.

Lack of Concentration

Completing your dissertation research in a timely, efficient manner depends on your ability to concentrate intensely without distraction. Such sustained concentration helps you maintain the focus required for the deep work of dissertation thinking, analyzing, and writing. Learning to concentrate fully is not easy and takes practice, commitment, and effort to develop. The outcomes, however, include the ability to learn more, master complicated tasks, and produce more in less time.

Two of the biggest problems that keep us from adequately concentrating—or focusing our attention—are interruptions and distractions. Tracy (2017) reminds us that "the attraction of distraction, the lure of electronic and other interruptions, leads to diffused attention, a wandering mind, a lack of focus, and, ultimately, underachievement and failure" (p. 86). While it's not possible to eliminate interruptions and distractions completely, with effort and willpower, they can be substantially reduced.

> To produce at your peak level, you need to work for extended periods with full concentration on a single task free from distraction.
>
> —Newport (2016)

One of the biggest challenges for dissertation writers is the temptation of the internet. While the internet offers an amazing array of resources to help make dissertation writing easier, it also poses a big problem in trying to focus attention on the task at hand; it takes a great deal of self-discipline to seek only what you need. Then there's the constant pings and rings of your smartphone interrupting your concentration. Even if you resist the urge to respond, you still lose focus and valuable time. In researching work interruptions, Dr. Gloria Mark, professor of informatics at the University of California, Irvine, found that when people move from one task to another, they work faster but produce less (Mark et al., 2008). Even short interruptions delay the time required for task completion. She reported that it takes an average of 23 minutes to regain focus on a task after being distracted.

Additionally, the lure of network tools such as Twitter, Facebook, email, blogs, Instagram, and infotainment sites also disrupts our momentum, leaving little time for deep thinking and unbroken concentration. Once distracted, it's difficult to reorient to the task.

In order to master the art of focused concentration, it will be necessary to change some of the deep-seated habits that could thwart your progress in completing your dissertation. This takes motivation and willpower. Below are some strategies that can help you develop your concentration stamina:

1. Create the Right Environment

It is important to minimize noise, as it is a big distractor and can greatly impact your ability to concentrate. Consider wearing noise-canceling headphones to blank out what might otherwise capture your attention. It's hard to stay focused when other people interrupt you, so when it's time for intense work, let people know you will be busy for a while and put up a "do not disturb" sign.

2. Set Aside Chunks of Time for Uninterrupted Work

Spending as little as 20 to 30 minutes of concentrated time can help you be more productive than two hours spent on a task filled with constant interruptions. One strategy to consider is to set a timer. This can help to keep you on target for a doable length of time. Work until the timer goes off, then do something else for a while. Then reset the timer and repeat. Consider using Google's timer. In the search box, type "timer 30 minutes" and hit Enter. Google sets a timer for 30 minutes and starts counting down. After 30 minutes, you will hear a beeping sound. The timer can be set for any length of time you desire.

3. Take Regular Breaks

Because our brain has a limited attention span, it is important to build in breaks during periods of intense work, as they have the power to recharge you and help you fight distractions. In the book, *Laser-Sharp Focus*, Jast (2015) shares information from researchers who recommend working in 60- to 90-minute periods. Her suggestions are to

- take a short 5- to 10-minute break every 60–90 minutes and

- take a longer 20- to 30-minute break every 2–3 hours. (p. 77)

This is an individual choice, of course; you can find your own optimum concentration/break times.

4. Avoid Multitasking

Multitasking is managing several tasks at the same time. Research findings are clear about the effect of multitasking on productivity. It has a negative effect! According to the American Psychological Association, work quality diminishes and error rate increases. In other words, when you multitask, it takes twice as long to complete a task and you make twice as many errors. Professor Earl Miller, a neuroscientist at Massachusetts Institute of Technology, found similar results in his research. He discovered that multitasking affects our mental clarity and makes us less efficient. He claims that when people say they can multitask well, they are deluding themselves. In reality, multitasking is a myth; our brain can only consciously focus on one task at a time. So, when you are working on a complex task such as dissertation research, it is to your advantage to avoid multitasking.

5. Take Control of Technology

In today's world, technology seems to be the biggest distraction that takes us away from focused concentration. The simple truth about

> To master the art of deep work, you must take back control of your time and attention from the many diversions that attempt to steal them.
>
> —Newport (2016)

technology is that it can control you rather than the opposite. If you are serious about developing the ability to focus your attention, then consider the following:

- Shut off all phones and notifications. The ring and ping of a smartphone disrupts your concentration which costs you valuable time in returning to your train of thought.

- Shut down your email program. Even though many of our emails are not particularly important, we often feel the urge to look at them immediately. You can establish specific times for checking and responding to your email.

- Limit your internet time. It's tempting to look for one more article to make your argument rather than sitting down at your computer to write about what you already researched. Because this seems to be a problem for many folks, you will find several access-blocking software options on the market.

These tools allow you to block those distracting websites that can kill your concentration. A few of these apps are included in the resources section at the end of this chapter.

Inner Resources Required for the Climb

The Backpack "Ten Essentials"

To keep any climb safe and enjoyable, preparation and good judgment are critical. Just as it's important that mountaineers recognize the awesome powers of nature for which they must be prepared, so must you understand the immenseness and complexity of the dissertation task and be prepared for it. Experienced mountaineers rely on a time-tested packing list, known as the "ten essentials," developed in the 1930s by a group of Seattle-area climbing enthusiasts. The ten essentials are what every outdoor person should carry at all times in his or her backpack to ensure survival. They include a map, compass, flashlight, extra food, extra clothing, sunglasses, first-aid kit, pocketknife, a fire starter, and water. The list is often expanded as the need arises.

These are mandatory items used in training for the Sierra Club's Basic Mountaineering Training Course certificate. When the unexpected happens on mountain trails, these items are truly essential. Climbing the dissertation mountain requires the presence of certain inner essentials to make it safely and successfully to the top. *Inner resources* are those intangible reserves that help you cope with problems and crises.

Especially in times of stress, it is the mobilization of these noteworthy attributes that helps remove or transcend the barriers you face along the path. In the words of German philosopher Friedrich Nietzsche, "That which does not kill me, makes me stronger."

The Dissertation Journey's "Essentials"

The dissertation journey requires innumerable inner essentials. Some of the dissertation writer's essentials are commitment, perseverance, stamina, positive mental attitude, courage, and the spirit of adventure. Although these six essentials are not the only ones, they are vital to your survival and ultimate success on the journey.

Commitment

Commitment is the willingness to do whatever it takes to achieve your goal. It is one thing to start something; it is quite something else to complete it. A genuine commitment is a promise you make to yourself to stick it out, regardless of the obstacles you face or how many times you are knocked down. You simply get up and press on. Becoming a doctor is only a dream until you commit the time and energy to obtain it. Imagine your name with a PhD or an EdD after it. Tom Flores, a National Football League coach, said, "A total commitment is paramount to reaching the ultimate in performance." Making a commitment gives you that extra ounce of courage that keeps you going during the tough times. Abraham Lincoln gave this advice: "Always bear in mind that your own resolution to succeed is more important than any other thing."

> The moment you commit and quit holding back, all sorts of unforeseen incidents, meetings, and material assistance will rise up to help you. The simple act of commitment is a powerful magnet for help.
>
> —Napoleon Hill

Perseverance

Perseverance is that attribute that impels you to go on resolutely, in spite of obstacles, criticism, adversity, fears, or tears, to overcome the inevitable discouragement and disappointment that accompany mountainous-type projects. It means putting in the hard work necessary to get the job done, even when you don't want to. Having spent relentless hours of effort over a long period of time, it's easy to lose heart and want to quit. This is when you dig deep into your inner reserves and keep going. Remember, there is a big difference between quitting and wanting to quit. The difference is between being ABD and becoming a doctor. High achievement is not reserved for those with innate talent or high IQs. It is dependent on desire and perseverance—on that extra effort. Students start their doctoral program expecting to be successful, but only those who are willing to pay the price and do what's required finish. There's an old saying: "A big shot is only a little shot who kept shooting."

Stamina

High-altitude climbing takes a tremendous amount of energy. It involves continual exertion and makes brutal demands on your legs, lungs, and heart. Stamina is what it takes! It's not optional. Writing a dissertation requires *stamina*—the strength to sustain long hours of work and yet maintain high performance. This is especially difficult when juggling the demands of a full-time job and sustaining family obligations while completing a doctorate. However, stamina is essential to surviving the journey.

Lessons from athletes can be of great value. For example, athletes learn to focus and trigger the relaxation response through deep and steady breathing techniques. Meditation and visualization techniques are extremely valuable in managing stress. You can get a second wind by taking time to refresh and rest your brain and body. Regular exercise also rejuvenates the mind and body and reduces stress. Good nutrition and a good night's rest are also vital to maintaining stamina. Staying emotionally healthy is easier if you are in good shape physically.

Positive Mental Attitude

A significant psychological discovery in the past 20 years is that people can choose the way they think. Henry Ford put it this way, "Whether you think you can or can't, you're right." A *positive mental attitude* is at the core of any high achievement and success in life. Try to avoid negative thoughts or negative self-talk whenever possible. These include thoughts such as "I don't have time now, so it's not worth starting" or "This will be too hard." It also helps to remove words such as *can't, never,* or *awful* from your vocabulary. They only keep you on a downward spiral. One technique that works when you hear yourself being negative is to say, "Stop!" Stopping these negative thoughts interrupts the downward spiral.

We know many doctoral students who focus on the difficulties, the unpleasant times, and the pains associated with struggling. Thus, they create for themselves a miserable experience. The students who possess a positive mental attitude look for the good in situations, even when it's hard to find. Their optimism is like a beacon that propels them forward, thus creating a joyful experience for them.

> Nothing in the world can take the place of persistence. Talent will not . . . genius will not . . . education will not. . . . Persistence and determination alone are omnipotent.
>
> —Calvin Coolidge

> Everything can be taken from man except the last of the human freedoms, his ability to choose his own attitude in any given set of circumstances—to choose his own way.
>
> —Victor Frankl

Courage

It takes *courage* to face the fears and doubts that often accompany writing a dissertation. During the initial stages of research, we've heard doctoral students openly express some of their biggest fears and anxieties about the dissertation process.

Here are the most commonly identified fears and anxieties:

- The negative impact on work and family
- Not measuring up to the task intellectually
- Lack of the necessary research skills
- Not enough time to do everything that needs to be done
- Fear of the unknown—don't know what they don't know
- Won't find an appropriate topic or an advisor
- Being overwhelmed
- Fear of criticism and committee rejections of their work
- Fear of failure
- Being emotionally vulnerable

These fears cause considerable anxiety at times which can result in self-doubt, insecurity, worry, and procrastination that keep you from doing your best work and moving forward. Sharing these fears and anxieties with others lessens their impact and helps you realize that everyone involved in the dissertation process has at least one or more of the same vulnerabilities. Facing them openly and honestly goes a long way toward bringing out the courage that sustains the most fearful.

Spirit of Adventure

Adventure is defined as (1) an undertaking usually involving danger and unknown risks and (2) an exciting or remarkable experience. The *spirit of adventure* means accepting a risk and standing up to your fear of the unknown—taking the path less traveled. The central motivation for adventuring is to attempt something you're not sure can be done, to go somewhere you're not sure you can go.

If you know what you want and why you want it and are willing to sacrifice and endure many obstacles to get it, then you have the true spirit of adventure. It's all about being willing to explore your own limits. Whether it's a physical adventure or a mental one, it is always replete

> Courage is the mastery of fear, not the absence of fear.
>
> —Mark Twain

> Intelligence and the spirit of adventure can be combined to create new energies and out of these energies may come exciting and rewarding new prospects.
>
> —Norman Cousins

with excitement, hazards, and triumphs along the way. Are you comfortable with ambiguity? Climbers must risk and face uncertainty. If you believe your journey to become a doctor is an adventure filled with new learnings and discoveries about yourself, others, and your field of interest, then your life will be transformed and you will contribute significantly to your world.

SUMMARY

This first chapter helped you understand the dissertation journey as a peak experience, a transformative and fulfilling life event. Completing the journey successfully requires understanding the sacrifices, stresses, and uncertainties you face along the path. It also requires knowing strategies to deal with the major hazards facing dissertation writers: procrastination, emotional barriers, writer's block, and lack of concentration.

Climbing the dissertation mountain safely and successfully requires inner essentials, such as commitment, perseverance, stamina, a positive mental attitude, courage, and a spirit of adventure. Commitment is the promise you make to yourself to complete the dissertation, regardless of the obstacles you face along the way. Perseverance means staying the course, even when you don't want to. Stamina entails the ability to sustain long hours while juggling work and family obligations and still achieving your goal. A positive mental attitude makes the difference between experiencing misery or joy along the path. Courage overcomes fear and self-doubt. A spirit of adventure means a willingness to explore your own limits and view the dissertation journey as a quest filled with new learnings and discoveries.

The next chapter familiarizes you with the mountain's terrain—the dissertation document itself. You learn about the dissertation's structure, format, and typical components; major steps in the process; and the individual's roles and responsibilities.

RESOURCES

MindTools, "Are You a Procrastinator?" by the Mind Tools Content Team

- https://www.mindtools.com/pages/article/newHTE_99.htm

Insight of the Day, Motivational Quotes

- https://www.insightoftheday.com/category/motivational-quotes

StayFocusd

- https://www.stayfocusd.com/

RescueTime

- https://www.rescuetime.com/

SelfControl

- https://selfcontrolapp.com/

The New York Times, "The Scientific 7-Minute Workout" by Gretchen Reynolds

- https://archive.nytimes.com/well.blogs.nytimes.com/2013/05/09/the-scientific-7-minute-workout/

The Dissertation Terrain 2

Any successful mountain climb, whether actual or metaphorical, requires knowledge of the terrain and the environment. The more knowledge, the better the chance of success. No mountaineer would begin a major ascent without a solid understanding of the unique nature of the mountain and its challenges, characteristics, and vagaries. So, too, must a dissertation writer fully understand the nature of the doctoral dissertation. This chapter describes the essence of the dissertation—its component parts, major steps in the dissertation process, and the roles and responsibilities of those involved.

What Is a Doctoral Dissertation?

A doctoral dissertation is a formal document that demonstrates your ability to conduct research that makes an original contribution to theory or practice. It is a partial fulfillment of the requirements for a doctoral degree (e.g., an EdD, DBA, PhD, PsyD, etc.). The term *original*, according to the Council of Graduate Schools (1991), "implies some novel twist, fresh perspective, new hypothesis, or innovative method that makes the dissertation project a distinctive contribution" (p. 15).

Several types of doctoral degrees exist, such as a DBA, DPA, EdD, PhD, PsyD, and so on. Historically, the PhD was seen as having a greater emphasis on research, whereas various other doctoral degrees were viewed as professional degrees. In recent years, depending on the university and the field of study, these distinctions have become somewhat blurred. The contemporary doctorate in the United States and internationally is structured as education that includes rigorous research experiences in the form of a dissertation that requires students to "generate new knowledge and to develop as individuals who use the power of scholarly inquiry to advance society" (Council of Graduate Schools, 2016, p. 20). It should also be noted that there are doctorate degrees (e.g., JD and MD) that don't require research in the form of a dissertation.

Increased globalization, proliferation of technology, big data, and the need to be agile in a rapidly changing world has given rise to new conversations about the nature, design, and products of the doctorate degree. There are a number of interested groups studying and debating how the doctorate degree should evolve in the coming years. These discussions are likely to result in a combination of new and current features of a doctorate degree, including research that connects scholarship to a greater sense of purpose within a larger context.

The dissertation document may vary in format, depending on the type of study, but essentially, all researchers define a problem with researchable questions, conduct an exhaustive review of the literature, choose an appropriate methodology, collect and analyze data, and present the findings and conclusions.

The length of dissertations can also vary. No set number of pages is required. It helps to follow the rule of thumb illustrated by this apocryphal story: A young boy, after meeting the towering Abraham Lincoln, asked the president, "How long should a man's legs be?" Lincoln answered, "Long enough to reach the ground." It's the same way with dissertations. The appropriate length depends on the degree to which you can responsibly and comprehensively answer your study's research questions and adhere to the policies of your institution.

Completing a dissertation represents the pinnacle of academic achievement. It requires high-level skills of discernment and critical analysis, proficiency in at least one research method, and the ability to communicate the results of that research in a clear, coherent, and concise manner. No previous writing experiences prepare you for such a challenging and rigorous task. Basically, it's a learn-and-grow-as-you-go process.

One efficient way to learn the dissertation terrain is to familiarize yourself with dissertations previously published in your chosen field of study. This helps you understand the format and style of accepted dissertations. Also read dissertations chaired by those individuals you are considering for advisors. In this way, you can obtain insight into that person's expected level of scholarship. Keep in mind that universities may vary in their approaches to dissertation structure and design requirements.

Typical Dissertation Structure

A dissertation's structure varies with the academic discipline and the methodology used. Chapter names may be different, but in one way or another, the questions displayed as follows are answered. Figure 2.1 is an overview of a typical dissertation's basic structure.

Figure 2.1   Typical Dissertation Structure

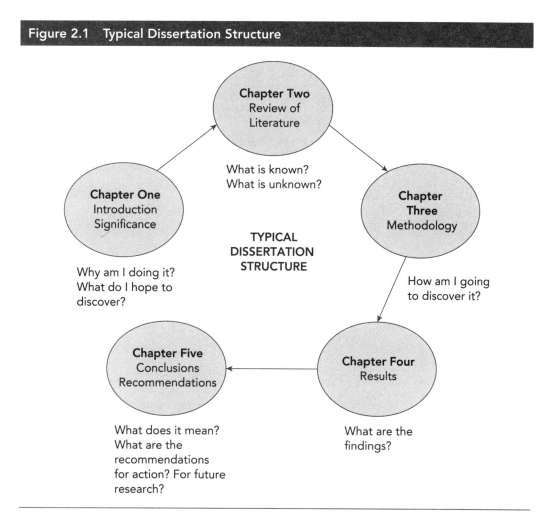

Most researchers try to resolve a specific problem and advance learning by answering the questions posed in Figure 2.1. Regardless of academic discipline, research usually follows the scientific method and has a similar basic format with some variations. To conceptualize your study, determine what the overall format will be. We ask our students to create an electronic file identifying the dissertation's major sections. This serves as an outline for the entire study. Students insert their writings into the individual sections within the file.

The following are sample formats of studies using quantitative and qualitative methodologies and some alternative formats. A quantitative study generally adheres to a standard found in statistical research studies, although the order of the various sections may vary.

Studies Using Quantitative Methodology: General Sample Format

Chapter 1 Introduction/problem statement
Purpose of the study
Research questions/null hypotheses/hypotheses
Significance of the study
Delimitations/assumptions
Definition of terms

Chapter 2 Review of the literature

Topics/subtopics
Summary

Chapter 3 Methodology
Type of research
Protection of human subjects
Population and sample (analysis unit)
Instrumentation
Data collection procedures
Statistical analysis procedures, including validity and reliability
Limitations

Chapter 4 Results
Findings

Chapter 5 Summary
Implications
Conclusions
Recommendations for further research

Varied structures can be seen in qualitative studies. However, they should exhibit a line of logic consistent with the assumptions inherent in the qualitative approach.

Studies Using Qualitative Methodology: General Sample Format

Chapter 1 Introduction

Topic and research problem

Rationale/purpose of the study

Guiding questions

Theoretical/conceptual framework

Significance of the study

Delimitations

Definitions

Chapter 2 Review of the literature

Topics/subtopics

Summary

Chapter 3 Methodology

Rationale and assumptions for the qualitative design

Type of design

Researcher's role

Protection of human subjects

Site and sample selections

Data collection techniques

Instrument

Managing, recording, and transcribing or presenting data

Data analysis procedures, including credibility and dependability

Limitations

Chapter 4 Methods for verification/trustworthiness

Coding process

Themes

Chapter 5 Results/outcome of the study

Discussion

Connections to previous research

Implications

Recommendations for future research

Conclusions

Alternative Formats

Model-Building Studies

Chapter 1 Problem and purpose

Chapter 2 Literature review

Chapter 3 Methodology

Chapter 4 Analysis of data

Chapter 5 Conclusion and model

Case Studies

Chapter 1 Problem and purpose

Chapter 2 Literature review

Chapter 3 Methodology

Chapter 4 Case studies

Chapter 5 Analysis of themes

Chapter 6 Conclusions, implications, and recommendations

Components of a Typical Dissertation

Your university likely has a format that you are required to follow. The following are some general items in each component.

Title Page

The title page—the first page of your dissertation—includes the title, the author, the degree requirements that the dissertation fulfills, and the date. The title of the dissertation is a succinct summary of the topic and generally should not exceed 15 words. Avoid unnecessary words, such as *A Study of.* The title includes key terms that readily identify the scope and nature of your study.

Copyright Page

Copyrighting the dissertation, although highly desirable, is optional. Unless your institution requires it, you don't have to formally register your dissertation with the U.S. Copyright Office in order to obtain copyright protection, but it is highly desirable to do so in case of any copyright litigation. Regardless of whether you formally register with the U.S. Copyright Office, a notice of copyright should appear on the page immediately following the title page. This informs others that your dissertation is not available for unrestricted use.

Committee Approval Page

This page contains the date of approval and the original signatures of your dissertation committee, the outside reader (if one is appointed), and the dean. By signing this page, they attest to the fact that they have read and approved your work.

Abstract of the Dissertation

The abstract is a brief summary of the dissertation that includes the problem, purpose, research questions, methodology, conclusions, and recommendations for action and future research. The abstract should be well organized, concise, and self-contained because it is often printed separately. A copy of the abstract is usually bound in the dissertation.

Table of Contents

The table of contents is essentially a topic outline of your dissertation, including all headings and subheadings, with accompanying page numbers. The following are generally included: acknowledgments, dedication, statement of the problem, review of the literature, methodology, analysis of the data, conclusions and recommendations, appendixes, and references. Each table of contents entry *must* correspond exactly to the title in the text. Consider preparing your table of contents ahead of time as a tentative outline for your study. It provides a good checklist for what needs to be done in writing the dissertation.

List of Figures, Illustrations, and Tables

Separate lists should be created for figures, illustrations, and tables. These lists should include the number and full name of each figure, illustration, or table as it is stated in the text. In addition, they should be listed in order of appearance in the text, followed by the number of the page on which the figure, illustration, or table appears.

Acknowledgment Page

Acknowledgments give credit to others for their guidance and assistance throughout the dissertation process. It generally recognizes the contributions of such individuals as committee members, other significant faculty, helpful colleagues, technical consultants, typists, or family and friends. Acknowledgments may also express gratitude for the use of copyrighted or other restricted materials.

Dedication Page

You may choose to dedicate your dissertation to a person or persons who have had a significant impact on your work. It gives you the opportunity to give special tribute to those who provided extraordinary support and encouragement. The dedication tribute may be placed at the end of the acknowledgment section or it may be a separate section.

Additional Components

It's important to review your university's dissertation requirements regarding additional components for inclusion (e.g., some universities require a brief CV [curriculum vitae] in their dissertations).

Chapter 1: Introduction or Problem Statement

This section of the dissertation gives you an opportunity to grab readers' attention and bring them on board with interest. It presents the problem addressed by the research, and it supplies a brief summary of the most relevant research and theory pertaining to the subject of the study. The problem statement should tell the story behind the research intent. It should provide the background to the purpose statement and research questions. In addition to the introductory problem statement, this section usually contains the purpose statement, research questions or hypotheses, the significance of the study, a definition of terms, delimitations/assumptions, and the study's organization. As an option, a brief summary of the introduction may appear at the end of the chapter. In addition, summaries may be used to conclude the subsequent chapters.

Chapter 2: Review of the Literature

The review of literature is a summation of pertinent literature directly related to your study. It provides a background for the important variables or concepts in your study and describes the similarity and difference between your work and that of other authors and researchers in the field. This review of the literature is traditionally your second chapter.

Chapter 3: Methodology

The methodology section describes in detail how the study was conducted. This chapter usually consists of the following sections: the type of research, the sample and/or population, instrumentation, data collection procedures, data analysis, and limitations of the study.

Chapter 4: Results or Findings

This section summarizes the data collected and details the statistical treatment of those data (if any). Tables, figures, or illustrations are used to report data clearly and economically. Findings are usually summarized at the end of the chapter. A qualitative study usually consists of narrative descriptions embodied in themes and patterns generated from the data.

Chapter 5: Conclusions and Recommendations

This section describes what the findings mean and what conclusions you drew from the research questions that guided your study. It details how your findings compare with those in the literature and with your conceptual framework. Included in this chapter are practical implications for professional practice as well as recommendations for further research.

References, Endnotes, or Bibliographies

A reference section at the end of the dissertation should list all works cited in the dissertation. A bibliography includes related material that you reviewed and studied but did not cite directly in the text. This helps the reader determine the scope of the research behind your dissertation. However, it should not include every article or book you read. There are distinct formats for citing references (including endnotes) that you may use depending on your university's preference. Once a format is selected, be consistent and follow it throughout the dissertation.

Appendixes

Materials that document important components of the dissertation that would be too lengthy, awkward, or distracting to include within the text should be included as appendixes. These materials might be raw data, letters of introduction to participants, long or complex tables, items required by your university's Institutional Review Board, and questionnaires. Such detail is useful to anyone trying to replicate your study in the future. Place items in the appendixes in the order they appear in the text. When more than one appendix is used, each must be designated by a letter (e.g., Appendix A, Appendix B) as well as by a title.

Major Steps in the Dissertation Process

The following is a brief description of the major steps needed to complete a dissertation. Procedures vary from university to university, and most universities distribute specific directions to their dissertation writers. Be sure to become familiar with these procedures as early as possible.

1. Select a Dissertation Topic

Deciding whether a particular topic has the potential for becoming a dissertation is one of the biggest challenges faced by doctoral students. There are no hard-and-fast rules in selecting a topic; however, the following are some criteria that will help in making your decision:

a. It needs to hold your interest over a long period of time.

b. It must be manageable in size.

c. It must have the potential to make an original and significant contribution to knowledge.

d. It should be doable within your time frame and budget.

e. It must be based on obtainable data.

f. It should be of interest to an advisor or committee.

2. Prepare a Prospectus

A prospectus is a 3- to 5-page overview of your study. It is basically a research concept paper that includes (1) background information about the topic with a brief commentary on pertinent literature, (2) a purpose statement, (3) research questions, and (4) appropriate methodology. This paper provides the basis for development of the proposal itself. It can also be used for discussions with potential dissertation advisors and committee members. Discussing your prospectus with a potential advisor or with potential committee members helps you obtain advice early in the dissertation process about the suitability of your topic as a worthwhile study and determine if the research questions and methodology are appropriate. A formal proposal expands on the prospectus and includes most of the components found in Chapters 1, 2, and 3.

3. Select an Advisor

Spend time getting to know those individuals who are available to be your advisor or committee members. Present your prospectus to those with whom you might like to work and get their views about the topic and proposed methodology. Once you select your advisor, work with him or her to focus and refine your topic into a manageable study.

4. Choose Committee Members

In consultation with your advisor, select your committee members. They should possess earned doctorates from an accredited institution, be considered outstanding in their field, be interested in your topic, have expertise in your topic or methodology, and be willing to spend time reviewing your dissertation document.

5. Complete and Present the Proposal

The proposal is usually written in several drafts in response to feedback from committee members. The proposal varies according to university guidelines and expectations. An acceptable proposal generally consists of Chapters 1, 2, and 3; the proposed research instrument(s) to be used in the study; and a reference list. Whether or not the proposal is written in the future or past tense depends on the requirements of your institution and the preference of your advisor. Generally, when all committee suggestions have been incorporated and your advisor concurs, a formal proposal meeting (also known as a *prelim*) may be held. In most instances, approval of your proposal becomes a contract between you and your committee. You are to satisfactorily conduct the study as described in the proposal, and the committee signs off on the proposal.

6. Conduct the Research

In this phase of the dissertation, you refine your instrument(s) per the recommendations of the committee and conduct, for example, a pilot test for a quantitative study to determine reliability and validity or a beta interview for a qualitative study. You collect, analyze, and interpret your data.

7. Write the Dissertation

The dissertation requires a high level of scholarly writing. You must be able to express yourself logically, clearly, and precisely. If you have difficulty with academic writing, consider hiring an editor. This can save you considerable time and make life easier for your committee by lessening the number of revisions needed. It enables your committee's comments to be directed toward substance rather than style. Editorial assistance for a dissertation is encouraged, but *only in matters of style, not content.*

8. Schedule the Final Defense

Your advisor typically leads the final defense meeting in which you present and defend your dissertation in the presence of the committee and other individuals permitted by your university. A final defense is usually considered a public meeting. At most universities, following the final defense, the committee certifies one of the following:

a. pass with no revisions,

b. pass with minor revisions,

c. pass with major revisions,

d. defense to be continued, or

e. fail.

9. Make Corrections and Resubmit the Dissertation

Incorporate all the changes resulting from the input provided at the final defense. Then, follow the special procedures outlined at your university.

10. Graduate and Become a Doctor!

Roles and Responsibilities

Doctoral Candidate

A *doctoral candidate* is usually defined as a student, accepted by the dissertation committee, who has successfully passed the proposal/preliminary meeting and who the dissertation committee then advances to candidacy. Becoming a doctoral candidate is a big step in the dissertation process, as it represents the committee's approval for you to begin collecting your data. It is the candidate's responsibility to get all forms signed in the proper sequence and to submit them to the appropriate individuals.

Dissertation Advisor

The dissertation advisor (also known as the *dissertation chair*) is the doctoral candidate's primary advisor during all phases of the dissertation process. The advisor is the leader of the dissertation committee and usually conducts both the proposal and final defense meetings. In conjunction with other committee members, the advisor is responsible for providing technical and content advice and assistance.

Dissertation Committee

Individuals who hold earned doctoral degrees from an accredited institution are invited to serve as members of the *dissertation committee*. The dissertation committee generally has three to five members, including the advisor. The committee's role is to provide different lenses through which to view your work. It is an opportunity to broaden your perspective by seeing your study from various vantage points. Candidates first select the dissertation advisor and, in consultation with him or her, select the other committee members. It is recommended that committee members reflect the range of expertise pertinent to the topic under study and the methodology likely to be used. Committee members are called on to advise the candidate throughout the process in areas appropriate to their expertise and interests. They also comment on written materials developed by the doctoral candidate. Committee members are responsible for evaluating and approving the proposal and the completed dissertation.

The Institutional Review Board or Human Subjects Review Committee

This committee is composed of a group of faculty members who review each research proposal for the purpose of safeguarding the rights of human subjects used for research purposes.

Additional Roles

There are a variety of different roles within each university related to the dissertation process. One important role is played by the department that processes the dissertation forms and makes sure that appropriate procedures are followed. Also, there may be university reviewers responsible for editing and reviewing the dissertation document for the proper style and format.

SUMMARY

The doctoral dissertation is a formal document that demonstrates your ability to conduct original research that contributes to theory and/or practice. Although variations exist, typical dissertations consist of chapters that provide background to the topic, a literature

(Continued)

(Continued)

review, a description of the methodology, findings, conclusions, and recommendations for action and future research. Major steps in the dissertation process include selecting a topic, preparing a prospectus, selecting an advisor and committee members, successfully completing and presenting a proposal, conducting the research, writing the dissertation, participating in the final defense, making corrections, and graduating.

Now that you know the dissertation terrain, it's time to consider the ethical issues in research. It is vital to be aware of the variety of ethical issues that arise in all phases of the dissertation process. The next chapter describes ethical issues, such as the rights of human subjects, the ethics of data collection and analysis, reporting findings, writing up research, and copyright law.

RESOURCES

CORE Services

- https://core.ac.uk/services

LexisNexis Uni

- https://www.lexisnexis.com/en-us/professional/academic/ nexis-uni.page

Purdue University, Online Writing Lab (OWL)

- https://owl.purdue.edu/

ResearchBuzz

- https://researchbuzz.me/

Microsoft Academic

- https://www.microsoft.com/en-us/research/project/academic/

Educational Resources Information Center (ERIC)

- https://eric.ed.gov/

Ethical Considerations in Research　3

The first step in the evolution of ethics is a sense of
solidarity with other human beings.

—Albert Schweitzer

Scholars are responsible for contributing to their field through rigorous research that incorporates sound methods while simultaneously
demonstrating high ethical principles. Ethical issues arise in all aspects
of conducting research. Such areas include attention to protection of
participants, data collection, data analysis and interpretation, respect
for the research site, writing up the research, and disseminating the
research. This section describes some of these central issues associated
with conducting and writing research.

What is considered ethical varies from person to person and from institution to institution. However, most professional organizations and
the various disciplines within the social sciences have established their
own standards or codes of ethics to guide their research activities. These
guidelines, according to Rossman and Rallis (1998),

> serve as standards for the ethical practice of research and are
> based on moral principles such as utilitarianism (the greatest
> good for the greatest number), theories of individual rights
> (the rights of the individual may supersede the interests of the
> greatest number), and theories of justice (fairness and equity).
> (pp. 48–49)

Institutional Review Boards

Colleges, universities, and other research institutions have institutional review boards (IRBs) whose members review proposals and approve research conducted at their institutions. Their main purpose is the protection of those participating in a research study, particularly around ethical issues such as informed consent, protection from harm, and confidentiality. Specifically, the IRB's role is to protect participants from "stress, discomfort, embarrassment, invasion of privacy or potential threat to reputation" (Madsen, 1992, p. 80).

If you decide to use questionnaires or conduct interviews, experiments, or observations, you need to submit a proposal to use human subjects to the IRB before actually conducting your study. Each institution has its own procedures as to when and how proposals should be submitted to the committee. Because your dissertation committee members may request changes in your original proposal, it is customary to wait until after your proposal has been formally approved by your dissertation committee to approach the IRB. The IRB's signed permission is necessary before you can collect data. When submitting your proposal to the IRB, be sure to provide detailed and comprehensive information about your study, the consent process, how participants will be recruited, and how confidential information will be protected.

The types of IRB reviews include exempt review, expedited review, and standard or full review. The IRB at your institution is guided by federal policies, which may be revised from time to time. University and college IRBs maintain policies and procedures, so it is important that you contact your institution's IRB to familiarize yourself with the required processes.

Clear ethical standards and principles exist regarding the rights of human subjects. They deal primarily with the impact on human subjects, including confidentiality and consent. It is critical that you carefully think through these issues when planning your research procedures and that you clearly articulate the nature and design of your research methods associated with study participants. The ethical issues involved in using human subjects in research are described in the section that follows.

Rights of Human Subjects

Protecting the rights of human subjects is a primary consideration when conducting research. The following rights must be granted to all participants in a research study.

Informed Consent

All prospective participants must be fully informed about the procedures and risks involved in the research project before they agree to take part. In addition, the principles of freedom and autonomy allow individuals to refuse to participate in the study or to withdraw at any time with no recriminations. In other words, their participation must be voluntary.

The following are the basic elements of informed consent that must be provided to each participant.

BASIC ELEMENTS OF INFORMED CONSENT

In seeking informed consent, the following information shall be provided to each subject:

1. A statement that the study involves research, an explanation of the purposes of the research and the expected duration of the subject's participation, a description of the procedures to be followed, and identification of any procedures which are experimental;

2. A description of any reasonably foreseeable risks or discomforts to the subject;

3. A description of any benefits to the subject or to others which may reasonably be expected from the research;

4. A disclosure of appropriate alternative procedures or courses of treatment, if any, that might be advantageous to the subject;

5. A statement describing the extent, if any, to which confidentiality of records identifying the subject will be maintained;

6. For research involving more than minimal risk, an explanation as to whether any compensation and any medical treatments are available if injury occurs and, if so, what they consist of or where further information may be obtained;

7. An explanation of whom to contact for answers to pertinent questions about the research and research subjects' rights and whom to contact in the event of a research-related injury to the subject; and

8. A statement that participation is voluntary, refusal to participate will involve no penalty or loss of benefits to which the subject is otherwise entitled, and the subject may discontinue participation at any time without penalty or loss of benefits to which the subject is otherwise entitled.

Source: U.S. Department of Health and Human Services (2010).

It is important to note that not all studies require informed consent. Rudestam and Newton (2007) pointed out that methodologies such as "secondary analysis of data, archival research, and the systematic observation of publicly observable data, such as shoppers in a suburban mall" (p. 276) may be classified as having minimal to no risk and require only exempt review. Your institution's IRB is an excellent resource as you begin this process.

Confidentiality

Addressing confidentiality is a primary responsibility of all researchers. The term *confidentiality*, according to Sieber (1992), "refers to agreements with persons about what may be done with their data" (p. 52). It refers to the identity of individual participants and to the information from participants. All participants in a research study must be informed about what happens to the data collected from them or about them and be assured that all data will be held in confidence. Once a study's data have been collected, no one other than the researcher should have access to it. Some statistical tests require correlating pretest with posttest scores. In this case, it is appropriate to assign each participant a numeric identifier or code that enables you to analyze the data. In addition, electronic and paper files that contain confidential data should be locked and stored in a place away from public access. This same technique of assigning a code or alphanumeric identifier can also be applied in qualitative studies.

> Research ethics is a very challenging subject which the research candidate has to face, and which if not addressed correctly may cause the result of the research work to be considered tainted or even invalid.
>
> —Remenyi et al. (1998, p. 115)

In addition to issues relating to informed consent and confidentiality, ethical considerations must also be taken into account around the methodological principles and procedures undergirding a research design. Ethical issues arise around all decision points in the research process—from the initial design planning to collecting data, accessing a research site, writing up research, and disseminating the results. Sensitivity to these issues and how you respond to them determines whether or not others question or trust the results from your study.

Ethical Issues in Data Collection

It is important to exercise responsibility in the processes you use to gather data for your study. In the social sciences, data are collected primarily through questionnaires, surveys, interviews, participant observations, audio and/or video, or technology-mediated approaches such as email or social media. Use of the internet and other communication technologies to gather data also requires permission from participants.

The following is a notice of implied consent used by a doctoral student to collect data using a web survey. When participants clicked on the link to the web survey, they were presented with the consent information and were advised that by continuing further, they were voluntarily agreeing to participate.

Welcome! Thank you for participating in this important research project.

All students adjust to college life in different ways. With this research, I hope to describe common thoughts, feelings, and experiences of university students. This study involves completing a questionnaire that typically takes 10 minutes.

Your participation is voluntary and your decision to complete or not complete the questionnaire will in no way affect your status or treatment at the university. By clicking on the "next" button below, you consent to voluntarily participate in this study.

Thank you!

Access to Research Sites

You may be collecting data from participants at a research site such as a school, a business, or a nonprofit organization. It is important that you respect the research site at all times. Yin (2014) asserts that you should "strive for the highest ethical standards while doing research" (p. 76). One of the main ethical concerns is the degree of sensitivity you display at the site and your interaction with the people in it. Most research sites have *gatekeepers*—people in authority who control access to the site. Examples might be a school principal, college president, company manager, or organizational leader. You must ask for and obtain written permission from them to conduct your study at their site.

Gatekeepers have concerns about the impact of your study on their organization as well as the possible disclosure of confidential information outside the organization. It is, therefore, your ethical responsibility to fully inform them about the ways in which your study may affect the work of the organization and its members. You should also disclose the ways in which the results of your study would benefit the organization. Through collaboration with these gatekeepers, you select those from whom you will collect data and under what circumstances.

Respecting research sites involves disturbing the everyday life and flow of activities as little as possible. Creswell (2004) suggested that participants be reminded

> a day or two before data collection of the exact time and day when you will observe or interview them. Stage the data collection so that they will feel comfortable responding, and schedule it at a time that is most convenient for their schedules. (p. 225)

It is important to remember that gatekeepers have a vested interest in protecting their sites. Your awareness and sensitivity to gatekeepers' concerns before conducting research on their sites will help you appropriately address any issues.

Recording Data

Audio and video recording raise significant ethical issues during data collection. To obtain greater accuracy, today's researchers may choose to record interviews. First and foremost, obtain permission from the participants and explain why you wish to audio or video record the interview or observation. In addition, explain how the recordings will be used and how they will be stored and ultimately destroyed according to IRB policies. Also, increase confidentiality by using alphanumeric codes or fictitious names.

Oliver (2008), in his book, *The Student's Guide to Research Ethics,* offered a strategy for relaxing participants while audio recording during an in-person interview. He recommended that the researcher

> place the tape or disc recorder within easy reach of the interviewee, and explain to them before the interview starts that they may use the pause button at any time . . . to consider their response to a particular question . . . or to reflect. (p. 46)

He further stated that participants could stop the recording if they wished. Oliver also suggested that interviewees be given the opportunity to listen to the tape at the end of the session and alter their words to more accurately express their views.

For interviews that are conducted using the phone or the internet, there are many technologies that can be applied. For instance, there are websites that have a feature that allow you to audio and/or video record the interview. Some researchers use email or a wiki to collect data. These technologies afford the researcher global access to participants, organizations, and communities.

Whichever means you select to collect data, it is important to remember to engage potential participants only after you receive written approval from your institution's IRB. Following IRB approval, you should provide information, secure consent, and obtain permission. Being transparent is key to ethical research.

Ethical Issues in Data Analysis and Interpretation

Data analysis is making sense of the data and interpreting findings appropriately so as to not mislead readers. The ethical issue is not about a researcher's honest error or honest differences of data interpretation; rather, it is in regard to the intent to deceive others or misrepresent one's work. Examples of such misconduct include using inappropriate statistical techniques or other methods of measurement to enhance the significance of your research or interpreting your results in a way that supports your opinions and biases. These are ethical issues of fabrication and falsification of data.

Fabrication is making up data or results, and *falsification* is changing data or results to deliberately distort them and then including them in your research report. According to Remenyi et al. (1998), "Any attempt to window dress or manipulate and thus distort the evidence is of course unethical, as is any attempt to omit inconvenient evidence" (p. 111). Remenyi et al. also pointed out that such strategies are not useful or rational because "even when hypotheses or theoretical conjectures are rejected, the research is perfectly valid" (p. 111). It is unethical to falsify results to make your study seem more acceptable and useful; negative results still add to the body of knowledge.

In research, the accuracy of the data is paramount. Therefore, you are obliged to employ validation strategies such as triangulation, member checking, audit trails, peer debriefing, and external auditing to check the accuracy of data. A list of resources that discuss ethics and their implications for data analysis is included in the resources section of this chapter. As an ethical researcher, it is your responsibility to be nonbiased, accurate, and honest throughout all phases of your dissertation.

Ethical Issues in Reporting Research Findings

Ethical researchers report results honestly and objectively. They don't hide negative results, engage in selective reporting, or omit conflicting data for deceptive purposes. For example, it is considered unethical to trim outliers from a data set without discussing your reasons. Roig (2006) addressed this issue by stating that

> researchers have an ethical responsibility to report the results of their studies according to their a priori plans. Any post hoc manipulations that may alter the results initially obtained, such as the elimination of outliers or the use of alternative statistical techniques, must be clearly described along with an acceptable rationale for using such techniques. (p. 35)

Another example concerns the ethics of generalizability. It is imperative that you not try to generalize the findings from your population to other populations or settings. Instead, make reference to this situation in the limitations section of your dissertation, usually found in the methods section. As an ethical researcher, it is your responsibility to accurately and honestly record and report your data using verifiable methods.

Plagiarism

Warning! Writing a dissertation that includes plagiarism can be hazardous to your career, your degree, and your reputation. Severe penalties can be levied against those who ignore copyright law or take it lightly. Plagiarism and copyright infringement are serious matters, one of the worst academic sins.

What Is Plagiarism?

Plagiarism is the theft of ideas. The definition of plagiarism stated by Booth et al. (1995) is the most comprehensive and helpful one that we've found in the literature:

> You plagiarize when, intentionally or not, you use someone else's words or ideas but fail to credit that person. You plagiarize even when you do credit the author but use his [or her] exact words without so indicating with quotation marks or block indentation. You also plagiarize when you use words so close to those in your source, that if you placed your work next to the source, you would see that you could not have written what you did without the source at your elbow. (p. 167)

Self-plagiarism is a form of plagiarism associated with using your previous writings and representing them as new. There are certain acceptable situations where you may duplicate a limited amount of your writing without citation, generally specific to methods such as instrumentation or analysis. However, a citation is required when using an extensive duplication of words. In all cases, duplication of material must conform to legal standards of fair use. Guidelines include that "the core of the new document constitutes an original contribution to knowledge in that only the amount of previously published material necessary to understand that contribution is included, and the material appears primarily in the discussion of theory and methodology" (American Psychological Association [APA], 2020, p. 256).

Basically, there are four ways in which you can be guilty of plagiarizing:

1. Using others' words or ideas without giving them proper credit

2. Using others' exact words without quotation marks or indentation

3. Closely paraphrasing others' words (even if you are citing the source)

4. Using your previously published writing as if it were new (self-plagiarism)

The third way is the most challenging for doctoral students writing their dissertations. The line between paraphrasing and plagiarizing is not always clear or straightforward, and it can cause inadvertent plagiarizing of another's work.

As a researcher, you must relate findings from the literature and from other researchers, requiring that you paraphrase or quote your sources. *Paraphrasing* is simply restating in your own words what others reported and then citing the source. How closely you parallel their words, even when correctly citing the source, determines the degree to which you may be plagiarizing.

Paraphrasing does *not* mean changing a word or two in another's sentence, changing the sentence structure, or changing some words to synonyms. If you rearrange sentences in these ways, you are writing too closely to the original—which is plagiarism, not paraphrasing. Booth et al. (1995) offered a simple test to ascertain whether or not you are inadvertently plagiarizing.

> Whenever you use a source extensively, compare your page with the original. If you think someone could run her

[or his] finger along your sentences and find synonyms or synonymous phrases for words in the original in roughly the same order, try again. (p. 170)

It is important to realize that words as well as ideas can be plagiarized, so be very careful when paraphrasing the work of others. If you are ever suspected of plagiarizing, it's extremely difficult to regain the trust and respect of your advisor or others who read your dissertation.

Ethics of Writing Up Research

In addition to planning and conducting ethical research, you must consider the ethics involved in writing it up. It is vital that you refrain from using biased or discriminatory language that infers inferior status to those with particular lifestyles or who belong to a particular gender, racial, or ethnic group. Scientific research and writing require that ethical and legal principles are employed to ensure accuracy and to protect the rights and welfare of research participants, including integrity, responsibility, and respect for changing culture and societal norms (APA, 2020). Rudestam and Newton (2007) also refer to the issue of bias-free writing. They advise writers to "stay current with language that is sensitive to diverse groups because what was acceptable terminology yesterday may not be acceptable today" (p. 282). To help eliminate biased language in scholarly writing, Rudestam and Newton offered the following helpful guidelines.

GUIDELINES TO HELP ELIMINATE BIAS IN SCHOLARLY WRITING

1. Substitute gender-neutral words and phrases for gender-biased words. A common mistake is the inadvertent use of sexist terms that are deeply entrenched in our culture, such as *chairman* instead of *chairperson*, *mothering* instead of *parenting*, and *mankind* instead of *humankind*.

2. Use designations in parallel fashion to refer to men and women equally: "15 men and 14 women," not "15 men and 14 females."

3. Do not assume that certain professions are gender related (e.g., "the scientist . . . he") and avoid sexual stereotyping (e.g., "a bright and beautiful female professor").

4. Avoid gender-biased pronouns (e.g., "A consultant may not always be able to see *his* clients"). A few nonsexist alternatives to this pervasive problem are to

    a. add the other gender: *"his or her* clients." This alternative should be used only occasionally because it can become very cumbersome. It is, however, preferable to awkward constructions such as *s/he, him/her,* or *he(she).*

    b. use the plural form: "Consultants . . . *their* clients."

    c. delete the adjective: "to see clients."

    d. rephrase the sentence to eliminate the pronoun: "Clients may not always be seen by their consultants."

    e. replace the masculine or feminine pronouns with *one's* or *your.*

5. Do not identify people by race or ethnic group unless it is relevant. If it is relevant, try to ascertain the currently most acceptable terms and use them.

6. Avoid language that suggests evaluation or reinforces stereotypes. For example, referring to a group as *culturally deprived* is evaluative, and remarking that the "Afro-American students, not surprisingly, won the athletic events" reinforces a stereotype.

7. Don't make unsupported assumptions about various age groups (e.g., that the elderly are less intellectually able or are remarkable for continuing to work energetically). (pp. 284, 288)

Style manuals are useful tools throughout the process of writing up your research. There are different style publications (e.g., American Psychological Association [APA], Modern Language Association [MLA], Chicago) associated with each academic field. Check with your dissertation chair, program, and institution to ascertain the required style. No matter which style manual your institution requires, standard ethics remain for conducting, reporting, and publishing research. "These long-standing principals are designed to achieve three goals:

- ensuring the accuracy of scientific findings,

- protecting the rights and welfare of research participants and subjects, and

- protecting intellectual property rights." (APA, 2020, p. 11)

In addition to the order and structure, a style manual often contains valuable information about expectations within your field, including ethics. We encourage anyone who is engaged in academic writing to keep their discipline-specific style manual close by.

Other Ethical Considerations

Copyright Law

Copyright protects original works of authorship, including both published and unpublished works. It gives copyright owners the exclusive right to reproduce their work from the moment of creation up to 70 years after the author's death.

Copyright law is an extensive, complex body of law. This section is intended to provide initial information only. It is intended to help protect your dissertation from unauthorized use and to protect others' works that may be used in your dissertation. The U.S. Copyright Office's website (http://www.copyright.gov) provides more comprehensive information.

Protection of Your Dissertation

Copyright is secured automatically when your work is created. However, to offset unauthorized use of your original work, we strongly advise that you place the copyright notice on your dissertation. Placing the copyright notice on your dissertation notifies others of your intent to protect your rights. You do not have to register your dissertation with the Library of Congress, unless you wish to do so. It is not a condition of copyright protection. However, there are advantages you should be aware of, which are addressed on the copyright website. The form of the copyright notice consists of three elements: (1) the symbol represented by the letter C in a circle as ©, the word *Copyright,* or the abbreviation *Copr.*; (2) the year of publication of the work; and (3) the name of the copyright's owner (U.S. Copyright Office, 2009). The elements need not appear in any particular order; however, usually they are in this order: © 2020 Roberts and Hyatt.

Your dissertation can be considered published as soon as it appears on the library shelf or online or is otherwise made available to the public. If you think you may want to profit from your dissertation by writing a book based on your dissertation, it is important to obtain formal registration of your work. Universities that require doctoral dissertations have guidelines and can assist you with this information.

Protection of Others' Work
Used in Your Dissertation

You need not obtain permission for those works in the *public domain,* that is, works with no copyright protection or those with expired copyrights. Academic honesty, however, mandates that you acknowledge all sources used in your dissertation, even those in the public domain. If you use copyrighted material in your dissertation, you must secure permission from the owner to include it, unless it falls under the doctrine of *fair use,* which allows limited reproduction of copyrighted works for educational and research purposes. This doctrine is rather complex and can have many interpretations. Miller and Taylor (1987) reported that most university style manuals permit "excerpts of up to 150 words, provided they do not constitute a major portion of the original work" (p. 46).

If you believe that what you are using falls under fair use, you need not obtain permission, but you must cite the source in footnotes or endnotes and in the references. Using copyrighted material in your dissertation without obtaining permission can be *copyright infringement* and is called *piracy* if you profit from it in any way. Both are serious infractions. Be sure to always obtain written permission from the author or publisher if you plan to use copyrighted material in your dissertation, such as tests, questionnaires, poems, figures or other artwork, or large excerpts of books. Madsen (1992) explained the process for obtaining permission:

> Send the holder of the copyright—usually the publisher of the book or article—a simple form listing the work, the pages and lines you wish to copy or quote, and the title and publisher of the work in which the material will be published. The form also should include a place for the copyright holder's signature. (p. 89)

This procedure will be necessary if you later decide to publish an article or write a book based on your dissertation. Should you wish to pursue more in-depth information about copyright law, refer to Strong's (1998) *The Copyright Book: A Practical Guide.*

The greatest gift you ever give is your honest self.

—Mr. Rogers

SUMMARY

This chapter focused on enhancing your understanding about ethical issues such as the rights of human subjects, data collection, data analysis and interpretation, reporting research findings, plagiarism, writing up research, and other ethical considerations such as copyright law, protection of your dissertation, and protection of others' work used in your dissertation. Ethical issues arise in all aspects of conducting research. It is incumbent on researchers to gain knowledge about their institution's administrative processes regarding research. Your dissertation chair and committee, along with the IRB, can provide valuable information to assist you in navigating the process. Additional resources that scholars find useful include a quality dictionary and a discipline-specific style manual.

The next step is to select an interesting, researchable topic to investigate. Chapter 4 provides some approaches to choosing your topic, where to look for potential topics, and criteria for topic selection.

RESOURCES

Academy of Management, Ethics of Research & Publishing Video Series

- https://aom.org/research/publishing-with-aom/ethics-of-research-publishing-video-series

American Anthropological Association, Ethics Resources

- https://www.americananthro.org/ethics-and-methods

American Educational Research Association, Professional Ethics

- https://www.aera.net/About-AERA/AERA-Rules-Policies/Profes sional-Ethics

American Psychological Association Style, Publication Manual of the American Psychological Association, Seventh Edition (2020)

- https://apastyle.apa.org/products/publication-manual-7th-edition

American Sociological Association, Ethics

- https://www.asanet.org/about/ethics

Modern Language Association, MLA Style

- https://www.mla.org/MLA-Style

Office for Human Research Protections, 45 CFR 46

- https://www.hhs.gov/ohrp/regulations-and-policy/regulations/45-cfr-46/index.html

Plagiarism.org

- https://www.plagiarism.org/

The Office of Research Integrity

- https://ori.hhs.gov/

U.S. Copyright Office

- https://www.copyright.gov/

PART II

Starting the Climb

Source: https://istockphoto.com/miljko

Every mountain top is within reach if you just keep climbing.

—Barry Finlay

Selecting a
Research Topic 4

The first major challenge in the dissertation process lies in selecting a research topic. Your choice determines how long it will take you to complete your study. For most doctoral students, it is an agonizing decision, mainly because of the uncertainty surrounding it. Has it already been adequately researched? Is it worthy of investigation? How original does it have to be? Is it manageable in scope? To know whether or not it has been researched or if it is important to the field, you must first immerse yourself in the literature base. It would not be worthwhile to conduct another study about a problem that has been sufficiently investigated unless, however, you conduct a meta-analysis, meta-ethnographic analysis, or literature synthesis. These research approaches synthesize findings across several studies.

Approaches to Selecting a Research Topic

In selecting a research topic, students sometimes use what Martin (1980) called "dreaming in a vacuum." He stated that some students believe great ideas come from moments of inspiration; students who walk in the park, backpack in the mountains, or sit in quiet places to contemplate learn a lot about parks, backpacking, and contemplation, but little else. Waiting for inspiration is not the best approach to topic selection. Research topics do not mystically appear. Some students attempt to find a topic that fits a set of already-collected data, a certain population to which the student has access, or a preferred research methodology. This backward approach is inappropriate and certain to irritate a potential advisor. The most effective and efficient ways to select a topic are the following:

1. Become steeped in the relevant literature.

2. Engage in discussions with faculty and other scholars in your field.

3. Write about your topic to help crystallize and organize your understanding.

Commonly, students consider three to five potential topics before finally settling on one. Scrapping a topic and starting over at least once is the norm.

Where to Look for Potential Topics

Dissertation topics rarely emerge out of the blue; you must proactively search them out. Here are some potential sources:

1. *Your own professional interests.* What excites and energizes you? What career goals could be enhanced by studying a particular topic?

2. *Faculty members, professional colleagues, and fellow students.* Listen to their suggestions about potential topics.

3. *Professional journals in your field.* This is where you can find out the hot topics of the day and for the near future.

4. *Librarians.* Ask them to help you run a database search on some topic of interest. Make a list of keywords and phrases to initiate the search. The results of a computer search should help you discover whether a dissertation is possible on this topic or whether the topic has been done to death.

5. *Dissertations.* Review previously written dissertations. Consult ProQuest Dissertations & Theses, from whom you can order dissertations of interest. Chapter 5 of most dissertations includes a section titled "Recommendations for Future Research." This is a gold mine of potential topics.

6. *Final defenses.* The discussions that occur during a dissertation student's final defense often suggest potential topics. Attend as many of these as you can. It opens your eyes to what happens during a dissertation defense.

7. *Current theories.* Have any new theories come out in your field or are existing theories being questioned?

8. *The internet.* A variety of sources exist on the internet.

9. *Conferences and seminars.* Often, these deal with current research in your areas of interest. Talk with presenters and authors to get their ideas about researchable topics.

10. *Outside agencies or professional organizations that conduct research.* Two excellent resources are the 10 National Educational Regional Laboratories and the American Educational Research Association (http://aera.net).

11. *Leading scholars in your interest areas.* Usually, authors and researchers eagerly talk with someone interested in their ideas and research. Most authors have websites where you can contact them to find out what they are currently doing and ask for their advice about potential studies.

12. *Your current job setting.* Are there problems that need solutions in your workplace? A dissertation is an extensive, scholarly endeavor and the topic should be one in which you have strong interest.

13. *References in your field.* All discipline areas have their own encyclopedias, handbooks, or yearbooks. You can access them on the internet by keying in your area (e.g., sociology, psychology) followed by the word *handbook*, *yearbook*, and so on.

HELPFUL HINT

Start a research topic file. As you get ideas about possible topics, save them to a computer file or as hard copies in a folder that you can review from time to time. Use this file to note helpful books and articles to read, good quotes, and so on. This helps keep your topic antenna up and alert for new ideas.

Some Criteria for Research Topic Selection

How do you know if your particular topic has the potential to become a scholarly dissertation? Most universities and doctoral faculty agree that the doctoral dissertation should be an original piece of research and significant to the field. However, what constitutes originality or significance is open to interpretation and usually differs among various faculty advisors. Madsen (1992) clarified the elusive term, *originality.* He claims that a topic must have the potential to do at least one of the following:

> Uncover new facts or principles, suggest relationships that were previously unrecognized, challenge existing truths or assumptions, afford new insights into little-understood phenomena, or suggest new interpretations of known facts that can alter people's perceptions of the world around them. (p. 38)

While there are no hard-and-fast rules for selecting a topic, there are some general criteria for considering a potential topic:

1. *It needs to hold your interest for a long time.* It takes longer than you anticipate to write an acceptable dissertation.

2. *It must be manageable in size.* Most students begin with a topic that is too large. Remember, you can't do it all. Your goal is to add a small but significant piece to the knowledge base and graduate! Save the Nobel Prize–level research to do as a postgraduate.

3. *It must have the potential to make an original and significant contribution to knowledge.* Can you find a hole, a gap, or a missing piece in the knowledge base that you can fill and would be useful to theory or practice?

4. *It must be doable within your time frame and budget.* Given your current situation, is it a feasible topic to undertake? Conducting a longitudinal study may not be advisable, based on your time to completion.

5. *It has to have obtainable data.* You must be able to collect new data or there must be available data for the study from an appropriate sample size in a reasonable period of time.

6. *It has not already been sufficiently researched.* There is no value to conducting one more study about a topic that has been researched over and over again within recent years, unless there is a new aspect that is of interest to the discipline.

7. *It should be acceptable to your advisor and committee members.* The signatures of these individuals determine whether or not you become "doctor."

8. *It has an impact on your present and future career.* Does it have immediate value to your present employer? Will your topic impress future search committees or enable you to publish?

9. *It has to have access to the population and/or sample from which you need to collect data.* Are the subjects available and willing to cooperate? What approvals are required?

Figure 4.1 is a way to make your own personal assessment of the preliminary topics you are most interested in pursuing.

Figure 4.1 Topic Criteria Assessment			
CRITERIA	**TOPIC 1**	**TOPIC 2**	**TOPIC 3**
Personal interest			
Manageable in size			
Significant contribution			
Doable			
Has obtainable data			
Not over researched			
Career advancement			
Accessibility			
Acceptable to committee			
TOTAL SCORE			

Code: 1 = Excellent, 2 = Good, 3 = Poor

We cannot emphasize enough the importance of making a concerted effort to become familiar with the literature and to talk with experts in your field. You cannot know for certain if the topic you desire is significant, nor can you have a clear notion about what is known and not known about the topic. Just because *you* don't know doesn't mean it is not known.

HELPFUL HINT

- A truism: You will encounter a wide range of opinions regarding the worth of any research topic. Some might think it outstanding, while others claim it has no value. Such a variety of opinions reflects each individual's particular interest, experience, or bias. The thing to remember is that you only have to satisfy your dissertation committee to pursue a topic that interests you.

- Another truism: Stubbornness in pursuing a dissertation topic no one believes worthy of research can lead to an ABD (all-but-dissertation) mindset. Time spent pursuing a lost cause can cost you valuable time and make it difficult to obtain an advisor.

Narrowing Down a Research Topic

The process of narrowing down your research topic can be challenging but it is one of the most important tasks you will undertake, assuming your goal is to finish your dissertation and graduate in a reasonable amount of time. Narrowing the scope of your research to a manageable size is absolutely critical. Scope reflects the boundaries of your study—the restrictions you purposefully impose to reduce its breadth and width. Scope is also known as *delimitations* and is usually discussed in the introduction or methodology chapter of a dissertation. (See pages 124–125 of this book for further elaboration). The scope of a study can also be explained in terms of its theoretical or conceptual framework. In what specific theory is your study grounded? What are the key concepts, subconcepts, or constructs upon which your study is focused? A detailed description of theoretical or conceptual frameworks can be found on pages 117–122 of this book.

Tips to Narrow Your Research Topic

- Select one facet or perspective within your topic that interests you the most. It's tempting to want to get your arms around all aspects of your topic. However, a narrow, well-defined dissertation will more likely be approved by your committee.

- Reduce the scope of your study by focusing on demographic factors such as age, occupation, ethnicity, gender, and so on.

- Select a smaller geographic unit of analysis.

- Select a specific time period for your study. Generally, the shorter the time span of a study, the more narrow its focus becomes.

Replication Studies

One strategy in pursuing a dissertation topic is to replicate a previous study. Replication usually means doing the study again with different variables. Often, students think repeating another's study is cheating and is taking an easy way out. It is quite the opposite. Knowledge accumulates incrementally through studies that build on each other over time, and replication adds strength, clarity, and validity to research findings. It may be important, for example, to know if the results from a previous study hold true in other settings or for other populations. You can make a valuable contribution by repeating an important study.

REMEMBER

Caution: It would not be wise to replicate a trivial study or one with a weak methodology or incorrect statistics.

Research studies may be replicated in several ways. You might choose to alter parts of the research design of a previous study. It would also be appropriate to add or subtract variables, restate the research questions, or alter the research instrument(s). You might replicate it in a different geographic area, with a different population, or using different instrumentation (e.g., an interview instead of the original survey). These modifications, provided there is justification, can help clarify existing results.

You may adapt the research instrument(s) to fit the new population under study. However, if you use the exact instrument from the previous study, you must obtain written permission for use from the copyright holder. You also must write a new literature review. Replicating a study is not nearly as easy as it seems.

In writing the dissertation, you must state a rationale indicating why replication is important (e.g., the previous study was conducted 15 years ago, there are updated variables that may influence the results, etc.). You must also acknowledge the replication and compare your findings with previous findings.

Replication Studies *Dos* and *Don'ts*	
DO	**DON'T**
• Highlight the need to replicate.	• Choose a topic for convenience.
• Cite replication.	• Appear to be plagiarizing.
• Contact the original author for agreement (put the agreement letter in the appendixes).	• Copy bibliography, literature review, or table format.
	• Confuse *adaptation* with *replication*.
• Make it your own study.	
• Bring a copy of the original study to your advisor.	
• Mention the replication in your purpose statement and in your findings and interpretation chapters.	

SUMMARY

Selecting an appropriate topic is one of the most important decisions you make on your dissertation journey. This chapter suggested some effective and efficient ways to select a topic and offered nine criteria to consider with a form (Figure 4.1) to assess the feasibility of each criteria. Replicating a previous study is often desirable and appropriate, since knowledge accumulates through studies that build on each other over time.

With knowledge of the dissertation terrain and a topic that interests you, the next step is obtaining expert guides to help you reach the peak. The next chapter concentrates on selecting and working with your dissertation advisor, committee members, and others responsible for guiding the dissertation process.

RESOURCES

Diigo

• https://www.diigo.com/

Lucidchart, Flowchart Software

- https://www.lucidchart.com/pages/examples/flowchart_software

Coggle

- https://coggle.it/

ProQuest Dissertations & Theses

- https://about.proquest.com/en/dissertations/

Scribbr, "How to Choose a Dissertation Topic: 8 Steps to Follow" by Shona McCombes and Tegan George

- https://www.scribbr.com/research-process/dissertation-topics/

Assembling Your Dissertation Team 5

Peak Principle:
Always Climb Fully Equipped

Climbing high mountains without being fully equipped is folly. Being fully equipped includes having expert guides. Exposure, high winds, treacherous ledges, bone-chilling cold, and unpredictable weather pose grave dangers for the novice climber. To reach the top and return safely, you must have knowledge of where, when, and how to climb. This kind of knowledge comes only from expert guides.

Expert guides are people who have already been where you want to go. They possess the wisdom of experience, know the terrain, and can assess the abilities and limitations of those being guided. Expert guides also inspire confidence and convey what must be done to accomplish the goal. For your survival, you must have absolute confidence and trust in their abilities and be willing to go along with their instructions.

Don't take the doctoral journey lightly, for there are multiple challenges and obstacles along the way. Selecting a dissertation advisor is the most vital decision you make; that's the person you rely on to help you face the challenges and overcome the obstacles. This person's primary responsibility is to guide your work. He or she becomes your "significant other" throughout the entire dissertation process. Thus, it behooves you to select wisely.

Selecting a Dissertation Advisor

The dissertation advisor's main role is to offer advice and counsel during each phase of the dissertation process. He or she helps you develop and refine your research topic and methodology, critique multiple drafts of each chapter of the dissertation, and guide you through the proposal and final defense meetings. In addition, your advisor provides encouragement, shepherds you through any roadblocks, and acknowledges your good work. However, his or her ultimate responsibility lies in ensuring that you produce a high-quality dissertation—one relevant and useful to the field and one that meets your university's standards of scholarly research. Your work reflects not only your own scholarship but also that of your advisor. Your professional reputation and that of your advisor and university are all on the line when someone reads your dissertation.

Criteria for Selecting an Advisor

Ongoing program evaluations conducted at our university found that the factors most helpful to students in completing their dissertations dealt with the student–advisor relationship. These factors, in order of their significance, were the following:

1. Student–Advisor Compatibility

While it is a good thing that your advisor likes your topic, *it is not necessary that the advisor be an expert in your topic.* Compatibility is often more important than expertise. However, it then becomes crucial that at least one committee member possesses expertise in your research area or methodology.

It's important that the person you select has a reputation for making sound, helpful comments/suggestions and returning written drafts in a timely manner. What is an appropriate turnaround time? A good rule of thumb is approximately two weeks. However, you should recognize that during very busy periods (grading deadlines, holidays, etc.), it might take longer. Your success depends on the quality and timeliness of the feedback you receive.

2. Advisor Understanding of Students' Needs

A good advisor is sensitive to students' needs yet demands quality work. It is important that your advisor shows interest in your personal welfare as much as the scholarly work you produce.

3. Advisor Accessibility

Accessibility is an important factor in your advisor selection. Professors are very busy people and have responsibilities for publishing and presenting their own research. Some have clinical practices or consulting commitments that can interfere with your progress. Additionally, some faculty may have nine- or ten-month contracts and may not be available in the summer. It is important that, to progress with your dissertation, you select a person willing and able to talk with you or meet regularly with you despite an excessive workload.

These results suggest some criteria you might use in considering your choice of an advisor. Before making that choice, take time to investigate and get to know potential advisors. You might talk with students who worked with a particular advisor, read dissertations chaired by an individual with whom you are interested in working, or take potential advisors to lunch and explore their interest in your topic.

Advisors exhibit a broad array of expertise, style, and personality and they have different expectations of advisees. In selecting a compatible advisor, an important criterion is the level of comfort you feel with that person. Does the person's style of working match your own preferences? For example, do you prefer working with someone direct and highly structured (who closely monitors your work, adheres strictly to timelines, holds regular meetings, etc.) or do you prefer someone more laissez-faire (who waits to be contacted by you, allows more leeway to follow your own leanings, expects a greater amount of independent thinking, etc.)? Do you need nurturing and more support along the way or are you a confident, independent worker? *The best advisor is one who can be your ally, advocate, and adversary when needed.*

REMEMBER

Most institutions and departments establish rules that govern who may and who may not chair dissertations. In some instances, only those individuals listed on an approved faculty list are allowed to serve as dissertation advisors. Other institutions arbitrarily assign an advisor. Because of the variation in practices throughout universities, we recommend that you learn the requirements of your university as soon as possible. Doing this helps you select someone best suited to serve as your advisor.

How to Approach a Potential Advisor

Generally, faculty can choose which dissertations they will or will not chair. Following appropriate etiquette improves your chance of obtaining the advisor you want. First of all, be adequately steeped in the literature related to your topic so you can talk intelligently about it. Also, prepare a well-thought-out prospectus to show a potential advisor. This document should clearly define the problem and methodology of your study. If done well, it provides insights into the clarity of your thinking and writing—something advisors look for in potential advisees.

Next, give your prospectus to a potential advisor and request an appointment to discuss it. Be direct about your situation—are you shopping for an advisor or have you decided on one? Don't expect an agreement to chair your dissertation right away, and don't feel rejected if you get a "no." Typically, faculty turn away students if they are overcommitted, not interested in the topic, or do not feel comfortable with the methodology or analysis procedures.

If you have difficulty finding an advisor to chair your dissertation, it would be helpful to obtain some realistic feedback from others and perhaps do some individual reflection to help you understand the cause.

Here are some common reasons why potential advisors turn students down:

1. *The topic.* It's too broad and ill defined, it may be trivial or poorly thought out, or they are not interested in the topic.

2. *Students lack academic skills.* The time and agony of working with poor writers, superficial thinkers, or those known for cutting corners are not worth the effort.

3. *Personal attributes.* Students who are antagonistic, abrasive, stubborn, or undependable always have a hard time convincing a faculty member to chair their dissertation.

You need to appraise your particular situation and decide where you might need to change. Perhaps you should adjust your behavior and attitude or get some professional help with specific skills you may lack.

Selecting the Committee

The dissertation committee usually consists of three to five members (including the advisor), depending on the type of degree and each university's policy. These members possess earned doctorates and are highly regarded professionals in their field. Select them for their ability to make specific and useful contributions to your study. These contributions might be expertise in the topic, methodology, or analysis used in the study.

The committee's primary responsibility lies in contributing new ideas, suggestions, and insights for each chapter. In addition, the committee judges the worth and quality of your dissertation and its defense. Committee members should participate actively in all phases of the dissertation process. Early involvement contributes to their sense of ownership in the dissertation and helps eliminate any surprises at the final defense. They should not be considered rubber stamps of the advisor.

Choose the committee in concert with your advisor. Always discuss prospective committee members with your advisor *before* issuing invitations to them to participate in your study.

The same criteria used to select an advisor are appropriate for selecting committee members, as they can be an asset to your progress. A compatible advisor and helpful committee members contribute greatly to your success in completing a scholarly dissertation.

Maintaining Productive Relationships with Your Advisor and Committee Members

Once you have selected your advisor and committee members, it is vital to maintain good working relationships with them. The quality of these relationships affects your successful progress toward finishing your dissertation in a timely manner. We offer the following as a guide for obtaining the help and support needed in your journey to become a doctor.

1: Clarify Mutual Expectations with Your Advisor

To build and maintain a positive relationship with your advisor, it is vital that you clarify your mutual expectations for working together. It would be wise to consult with previous advisees to understand, from their perspective, the expectations and good strategies they used to work harmoniously and productively with your advisor. We recommend holding an open and honest meeting with your advisor and obtaining answers to some of the following questions:

1. What are your preferences about submitting drafts—email, hard copies, or both?

2. Would you prefer to comment on rough drafts or wait until a more polished draft is written?

3. How much time do you typically need to provide feedback?

4. How would you like for us to communicate regarding questions and meetings—phone, email, text, or another way?

5. What are your preferred times to meet?

6. How would you like me to communicate with other committee members? (Miller, 2009)

In addition to understanding your advisor's preferences and expectations, you need to openly share your expectations for completing the dissertation. For example, do you have a burning need to graduate within a specified time? Do you have a particular window of time to collect your data? Are you getting married or having a baby? If so, you need your advisor's support to adjust your timeline for completing your study. It is also a good idea to share your desires about the kind of feedback most helpful to you as well as how often you would like to meet—as needed or at regular intervals.

Dissertation Timeline

We highly recommend mutually creating a dissertation timeline with your advisor as soon as possible. Developing a realistic timeline for completing the tasks that culminate in a successful dissertation keeps you focused and on track to meet specific milestones toward meeting your goal of becoming a doctor.

First, you need to identify specific dissertation milestones and assign dates to each. To create your timeline, it is best to start with the end date (i.e., submission) and work backward. To be on the safe side, plan to submit your dissertation at least two weeks before the final deadline to protect you against delays caused by unanticipated problems. (See pages 84–85 for examples of a Gantt Chart [Figure 6.1] and a dissertation timeline in the format of a Dissertation Completion Schedule [Figure 6.2].)

2: Always Submit Drafts of Your Best Work

Resist the temptation to submit drafts that are not carefully thought out, organized, or well written. It is inappropriate to throw something together in the hope that it gets approved or that your advisor will think and edit for you. With a polished draft, your committee can focus its feedback on substance rather than style and format. Take time to carefully proofread each page. You can pick up many mistakes by reading it aloud to yourself or to another. It also helps to have a critical friend read it over before you submit it to the committee. Very often, committee members' initial impressions are lasting ones. Sternberg (1981) said it well:

> It has been my experience as a dissertation adviser and editor/consultant for several publishers that the reader's attitudes and appraisal of a manuscript are disproportionately shaped by the first draft which comes to his [or her] attention. If the first impression is unfavorable, successive drafts—even substantially revised ones—never quite erase the memory or smell of the first stinker. (p. 131)

Sloppy, careless work is unappreciated, and it reflects an attitude that you willingly cut corners and don't care about quality. It also shows a lack of respect for your committee's time. Always do your best work with each draft you submit.

3: Accept Criticism with Grace and Nondefensiveness

Your dissertation should reflect scholarly research and, as such, requires quality thinking and writing that is clear, concise, and cohesive. Expect to make multiple revisions to create such a document. It is critical that you accept your committee's feedback without getting your feelings hurt or being defensive. Develop professional maturity and remember: The committee's job is to provide comments and suggestions that strengthen your study and ensure that it adheres to your university's high standards. Show that you are teachable, flexible, and open to the committee's advice.

4: Always Incorporate Your Committee's Recommendations for Revisions

Committee members spend considerable time reading and critiquing your drafts. Usually, they are conscientious about making suggestions for improvement. It is not okay to ignore their suggestions. They trust you to incorporate their ideas into your study. Be sure to indicate on your return drafts where you incorporated their suggestions (boldfaced, colored/highlighted, italics, or in a personal note to them). Often, suggestions are negotiable. If you disagree with any of the changes suggested by a committee member, contact your advisor to discuss how to proceed. With your advisor's blessing, call that committee member to discuss the situation. Present your ideas persuasively and with tact and diplomacy. Show that you are flexible and open to their opinions rather than defensive of your own position. Such an approach resolves your differences in an amiable fashion.

5: Respect Your Committee's Time Constraints

Faculty are busy people and must be given sufficient lead time to respond to drafts and inquiries. Don't demand instant turnaround or immediate appointments. However, it is reasonable to ask when a response might be forthcoming. A comment that all advisors dread hearing is, "I realize I've taken six months to revise Chapter 1, but would you be able to read it by tomorrow?" One professor explained, "Bad planning on your part does not constitute an emergency on mine." Do keep to your timeline as much as possible. Often, faculty members make decisions about adding additional advisees based on when you plan to complete your dissertation.

6: Keep a Positive, Cheerful Attitude

Enthusiasm engenders enthusiasm and makes working with you so much more pleasant. Your committee wants you to have a positive experience. If you appear morose and whiny, it negatively affects your working relationship. Even if you don't feel positive and cheerful, fake it!

7: Take the Initiative but Expect Guidance

An important goal in writing a dissertation is developing the ability to work independently. You need advice and counsel along the way, but it is your responsibility to determine the direction of the research, manage your time, and persist in getting the work done. Take control of your own dissertation. What do you want to know? What is important to you? A good advisor encourages you to make your own decisions; after all, it is *your* dissertation. Don't wait to be told what to do. It delights your advisor when you bring fresh ideas and new insights and perspectives about your study. Keep self-sufficiency and dependence in proper balance. It's up to you to succeed.

8: Maintain Contact

Schedule regular meetings (at least once a month) with your advisor to discuss progress and to get advice on specific problems you may be having. It helps keep you in your advisor's memory, maintains the relationship, and shows your commitment to completing the dissertation in a timely manner.

With your advisor's approval, consider making regular progress reports to your committee. One effective way to do this is to complete the following and send it to your committee members:

Date: _____ Student Name: _____

Dissertation/Thesis Title:_____

_____

Items Initiated: _____

_____

Items in Progress: _____

Items Completed:_____

_____

Questions:_____

_____

In addition to sending a written progress report by email or as preferred by the advisor and committee, you should also make contact every month or as agreed to by your advisor and committee to keep communication channels open.

Be sure to seek advice when you need it. Often, students inhibit themselves in this regard and don't want to appear ignorant or incompetent. It is easy for advisors to overestimate the depth of their students' knowledge. Just don't be a pest! Remember to share the joy of discovery as well as the obstacles overcome.

Adhering to these eight guidelines creates a more harmonious relationship with your advisor and committee members and ensures a relationship based on mutual respect and shared responsibility.

Be sure to select committee members who are collegial and compatible with each other. Professors have political, ideological, and intellectual differences that, if in direct opposition, could create conflict within the group and interfere with completing your dissertation in a timely manner. Considering committee compatibility along with clarifying relationships, expectations, and procedures helps prevent problems and conflicts that might arise among the group.

Choosing Outfitters and Bearers (Other Specialized Consultants)

In addition to expert guides, difficult climbs also require outfitters and bearers. You can only reach a high goal with help from other people. Be smart and use all the resources available to you. There are consultants (editors, statisticians, research specialists, etc.) you can call on for expert help and advice. There are campus services available for your use as well as supportive, caring faculty and student peers eager to help you on your way. Going it alone can be inefficient and costly—it may even cost you your degree. Choose your guides and mentors carefully and then heed their advice and counsel.

Technical Assistance

Often, students require assistance with the technical aspects of writing a dissertation. Getting help with questionnaire design and statistical analysis is reasonable. Unless you were the valedictorian of your statistics class, it behooves you to consult a statistician; however, it is vital that you know enough about statistics to understand the statistician's advice. An experienced statistician can assist you with analysis techniques, interpretation of the numbers generated, table presentations, and technical writing. He or she should act as a tutor to help you understand why a particular test was used and what the results mean. However, you are responsible for understanding your statistics and defending their use at your final defense.

Writing Assistance

Consider using an editor throughout the dissertation process. Committee members do some editing; however, their primary role is to assist you with conceptual clarity. They appreciate receiving drafts that pass the literacy test. An editor can be someone skilled in grammar who understands dissertation-style writing. If your writing leaves a bit to be desired, then definitely hire a professional. It saves you hours of grief and a multitude of drafts. Just remember that editorial assistance for a dissertation is permissible and encouraged but *only in matters of style, not content.*

Word Processing Typist

It takes a tremendous amount of skill to prepare tables, figures, and so forth and to type the dissertation manuscript in the appropriate style format. The final document has to be *precisely* in the style required by your university. Most students do not possess this expertise nor do they have time to learn it. Therefore, our advice is *don't do your own final copy.* Hire a professional to complete the copy for final defense and for delivery to the university. This saves you much anxiety, time, and money. Be sure to contract with a typist early in the dissertation process. Provide an approximate date when you will hand over your manuscript.

Where to Locate Specialists

Check with your university to see if there is a list of experts available to assist you. Also, the Association for the Support of Graduate Students has a database of professional consultants (editors, word processors, and writing consultants). The names are arranged according to expertise areas and geographic location. You can click on a name and view detailed information, including services and hourly rates. Another good way to locate reliable technical specialists is to simply ask prior dissertation students and university faculty whom they know and recommend. Try to get at least two names so you can have a choice and not feel tied to someone with whom you may not be compatible.

Once you have a list of names, contact them. Let them know who recommended them and share your timetable for completing the dissertation. Also, let them know what kind of help you need and find out if they have the time to assist you and what they charge.

Dissertation Support Groups

The traditional African proverb, "It takes a village to raise a child," can be applied to dissertation writers. The fact that only about 40 percent to 50 percent of doctoral students complete their degrees is a consistent research finding. Even though the reasons vary considerably, the issue of support—kind and amount—usually affects this attrition in some way. Sources of support come from family, other students, consultants, coaches, and faculty. You enhance your chance of obtaining your doctorate when you deliberately seek out all sources of support.

At the beginning of this chapter, we described the role of advisors, committee members, and other consultants and how they support you along the journey. An additional support that can expand your "village" and make a considerable contribution to completing your dissertation in a timely manner is a peer dissertation support group.

Joining or creating a support group provides both emotional and academic support during the dissertation process. Researching and writing a dissertation can be lonely and isolating. For the most part, it is a solitary journey. It's easy to drop out when you feel as if no one understands or cares. Surrounding yourself with people who empathize and support you can be a valuable asset.

Few people outside your doctoral peer group understand what you're going through emotionally or have a clue about how to help you academically. Support group members understand your dilemmas and frustrations and help lift your spirits. They provide an ear to listen, a shoulder to cry on, and a foot to boost you back on track when necessary. They help you when you're stuck. They are your cheering squad and reliable critics who contribute valuable insight and suggestions (from conceptualizing a research topic to improving your written drafts).

Critical Decisions

There are no clear-cut rules for creating a viable dissertation support group. Each group must determine its own goals, expectations, and working procedures. But before jumping into a group or attempting to create one, some critical decisions should be made if the group is to survive and benefit all members. Here are some questions to consider:

- **How many members should there be?**

    We feel that the maximum number should be four to six members. It's an optimal size to obtain diverse viewpoints and to give and receive feedback, not to mention agreeing on meeting times and locations. It's a good idea to select members who have similar commitments to the group, as time must be set aside to read, reflect, and comment on others' work.

- **How often and for how long should the group meet?**

  We believe a good interval between group meetings is once every month in order to accommodate group members' other obligations. We also believe you should keep your meetings to around 90 minutes or two hours max. Limiting your time forces you to stay on task.

- **Should the group have a formal leader, rotate leadership, or be leaderless?**

  We recommend selecting a facilitator/convener who sends reminders, starts the meeting on time, and keeps it on track. This creates a more efficient and productive meeting and helps members feel their valuable time is well spent.

- **What are the group's goals? What does each person want from the group? (Is the group primarily academic—focused on critiquing written drafts or discussing methodology? Is it primarily for support—focused on providing social and emotional support?)**

  The ultimate goal to keep in mind is helping all group members maintain steady progress toward completing their dissertation and earning their doctorate.

- **What norms or group guidelines should be established?**

  It is critically important that group members collectively develop and agree on group guidelines (i.e., stick to agreed-upon time limits, honor commitments, be on time, provide food if meeting in-person, etc.) and refer to them regularly.

- **What format should meetings follow?**

  In our experience, most groups prefer setting aside a brief time for socializing and checking in with each other about milestones achieved, triumphs, frustrations, and so on. For example, an opening question might be, "What small success have you had since we last met? What challenges did you overcome in accomplishing your goal?" Consider blocking out equal amounts of time for each person to talk about whatever is important to them—to share obstacles that hindered progress or dissertation victories or to ask for input about a problem they are facing, feedback on a specific chapter, or advice.

- What kind of feedback should be given and how much time is expected for providing feedback?

  Giving and receiving feedback is the core of the peer dissertation group experience. Each person needs to commit to setting aside adequate time to give focused feedback. Additionally, it is important that feedback be honest, thorough, and couched in a positive, respectful way and include suggestions for improvement. How individuals offer feedback is crucial to building and maintaining trust among the group. When receiving feedback, be sure to listen attentively to all of it before asking any clarifying questions. It is important that you are not defensive; your colleagues are there to help you write better and finish your dissertation in a timely manner.

REMEMBER

Successful support groups not only optimize their time on task, but they also remember to

- laugh together, maintain a sense of humor, and share funny stories;

- celebrate each other's victories; and

- not take themselves so seriously that they lose sight of the joy in climbing the dissertation mountain.

Other successful strategies students use at our university are contingency enforcement and timeline monitoring. *Contingency enforcement* means that when a group member fails to accomplish a stated dissertation goal or task, meet a specific deadline, or attend a meeting, the group enforces that person's contingency plan. The plan might be as simple as buying a lottery ticket for the group.

These support groups bond students in significant and touching ways. They frequently attend each other's final defense and take notes so their friend can concentrate on the feedback received. Group members often become lifetime friends who creatively celebrate each other's successes even beyond the dissertation years. They have great times together, laughing and sharing the joys and sorrows of dissertating. Some groups stay together until the last person graduates, having faithfully attended each other's graduation ceremony and party.

Students also help each other monitor dissertation timelines. They bring to the support group meeting their projected timeline for completing the dissertation. The timeline consists of all major tasks to be completed, from obtaining an advisor to making final revisions. They are held accountable by the group for staying on that timeline.

HELPFUL HINT

Select group members carefully. There are certain personality types that make group work difficult and tiresome. Domineering types; shy, retiring types; and negative thinkers place considerable stress on a group. Also, there are those who are extremely needy emotionally and drain the group's energy by asking everyone to help them cope. For the group to be satisfying, all participants need to both give and take equally—to critique and be critiqued.

Other Considerations

Rather than joining a support group, consider working with one other person—a dissertation buddy. Someone you know well and with whom you are very compatible could be more efficient than a larger group. You might consider creating a virtual support group. With compatible software and computer skills, the same amount of support could be given online through chat rooms, online editorial critiques, online coaches (faculty or competent alumni), and so on.

SUMMARY

Selecting an advisor and committee members is one of the most vital decisions you make. Ideally, these individuals should like your topic, make helpful suggestions, return drafts in a timely manner, be accessible, and hold you accountable for quality work. In this chapter, we suggested eight rules to help you maintain a good working relationship with your advisor and committee members and offered guidance in observing appropriate etiquette when approaching a

(Continued)

(Continued)

potential advisor. Other available resources to help you complete the dissertation are statisticians, editors, typists, and so on.

To expand your dissertation support, we suggested that you consider joining a peer dissertation support group. It can provide both emotional and academic support during the dissertation process. However, before creating or joining a dissertation support group, consider the following: the number of members, time schedules, leadership roles, individual needs, group goals, group norms, meeting format, and appropriate feedback. In lieu of a dissertation support group, we suggest working with a dissertation buddy or creating a virtual support group.

Preparation for the beginning of your climb thus far included filling your backpack with the inner essentials, identifying a topic to research, and selecting expert guides, outfitters, bearers, and a dissertation support group.

Before making your climb to base camp, you should pay attention to organizing yourself. The next chapter provides helpful hints on organizing your workspace and your time, working smart, and maintaining balance in your life.

RESOURCES

The ABD (All-But-Dissertation) Survival Guide

- https://www.abdsurvivalguide.com/

Google Drive

- https://www.google.com/drive/

"Starting an Effective Dissertation Writing Group" by Dr. Sohui Lee and Dr. Chris Golde

- https://my.vanderbilt.edu/danielatorre/files/2013/12/ Writing-Group-Handout.pdf

Zoom

- https://www.zoom.us/

Skype

- https://www.skype.com/en

Adobe Connect 12

- https://www.adobe.com/products/adobeconnect.html

Organizing and Planning for Success 6

Success is focusing the full power of all you are on what you have a burning desire to achieve.

—Wilfred A. Peterson

Successfully completing your dissertation requires organization and planning. Working hard is not enough, you must also work smart. *Working smart* means organizing a place conducive to writing and developing a time schedule to which you faithfully adhere, even if you lack inspiration. Knowing yourself and the peaks and ebbs of your energy patterns is essential to efficiently getting the job done. Working smart also requires maintaining balance in your life. Today, many doctoral students are married with children and hold full-time jobs, making it essential to balance dissertation activities and other life obligations. This chapter offers suggestions for organizing your workspace, your time, and yourself for effective dissertating and for maintaining balance in the process. Think of these suggestions as options. Try them out to see which ones work for you.

Organize Your Workspace

It is extremely important that you find a suitable place for dissertating where you can be productive. Determine where you do your best work and plan to be there each time you work on the dissertation. Your dissertation workspace may be your office at work, your office at home, or a separate area in your home designed exclusively for your dissertation work. It should be quiet, private, and free of interruptions and distractions such as posters, TV, fish tanks, portraits, and pleasure books—a place to help you focus and maximize your attention. Let the answering machine take phone messages while you work. If music helps you write, then keep CDs or your iPod handy. Relegate to this office only those activities related to the dissertation—no writing letters, paying bills, or surfing the internet. Having a single-minded focus makes you much more efficient. Wherever you work, make sure you have the following:

- Appropriate technologies
  - Reliable computer/laptop and printer
  - Auxiliary data storage devices (flash drives, etc.). Some of the new-generation compact high-speed portable hard drives let you take your data with you when you're out and about.
  - Scanner (to transfer text directly to your computer)
  - Digital tablet
- Comfortable, ergonomic chair
- Sturdy, decent-sized desk. Consider purchasing a height-adjustable standing desk. It helps you get up and move while you work. Sitting at your desk for hours at a time can lead to back pain and posture problems.
- Good lighting (the latest research recommends bluish-white light, which helps you stay more alert)
- Appropriate reference materials (dictionary, thesaurus, style manual, etc.)
- Necessary materials (printer ink cartridges, etc.)
- Bookcase and safe technology storage (e.g., backup drives)
- As required by the institutional review board for storing confidential information and keeping data secure, you will need a password-protected computer file for technologically stored information or a locked file cabinet if you are keeping hard copies.
- File folders or a computer with online files
- Writing materials (pens, pencils, sticky notes, tablets, etc.) if you prefer to keep hard copies of notes
- An ideas notebook (online or hard copy) to jot down ideas that come to you

It is also important to be aware of environmental noise that can rob you of maximum productivity. Things like "background music, city sounds, and people's conversations lead to a decrease in performance" (Davis, 2015, p. 126). So, for dissertators, busy, noisy coffee shops may not be the best place for completing tasks efficiently. An organized workspace, devoid of distractions and dedicated exclusively to your dissertation study goes a long way toward maintaining optimum efficiency.

Organize Your Time

Because no deadlines are imposed on you while writing the dissertation, time can escape quite easily. Completing a dissertation requires that you manage your time well. Realistically assess how much time you can devote to your dissertation study. It is a big challenge to *find time* in an already-busy daily schedule. The reality is that you must *make time*. Those who don't will relegate themselves to the title ABD (all-but-dissertation).

Planning and scheduling time are the keys to making things happen. *Planning* is deciding what to do. *Scheduling* is deciding when to do it—picking the time to do the activities. It is more like a commitment, whereas planning is the intention. Scheduled things tend to happen. To be truly efficient, create at least three scheduling plans. First, design an overall dissertation timeline, which helps you see the big picture and keeps you on track. Second, create a time schedule to which you commit so many hours each day or week. Third, create a to-do list—a reminder of the tasks that need to be done each day. The following describes these three techniques and offers some recommendations to make them work for you.

1. The Dissertation Timeline

Your dissertation timeline can take several forms. One useful form is called the Gantt chart—a method for creating a dissertation timeline; it can be as detailed as you wish (see Figure 6.1). To construct a Gantt chart, list the major phases or specific activities of the dissertation down the left side of the chart. Across the top, list the time for completing the entire dissertation process. Then, create a bar graph that shows the beginning and ending times for each major phase or activity. When creating this long-range plan, it helps to work backward from your desired date of graduation. When do you need to turn in the dissertation in order to meet graduation deadlines? To do that, when would you need to defend your dissertation? To do that, when would you need to get it to the committee? Two online Gantt-creating tools are listed in the resource section at the end of this chapter.

> Don't say you don't have enough time. You have exactly the same number of hours per day that were given to Helen Keller, Pasteur, Michelangelo, Mother Teresa, Leonardo da Vinci, Thomas Jefferson, and Albert Einstein.
>
> —H. Jackson Brown Jr.

Figure 6.1 Gantt Chart

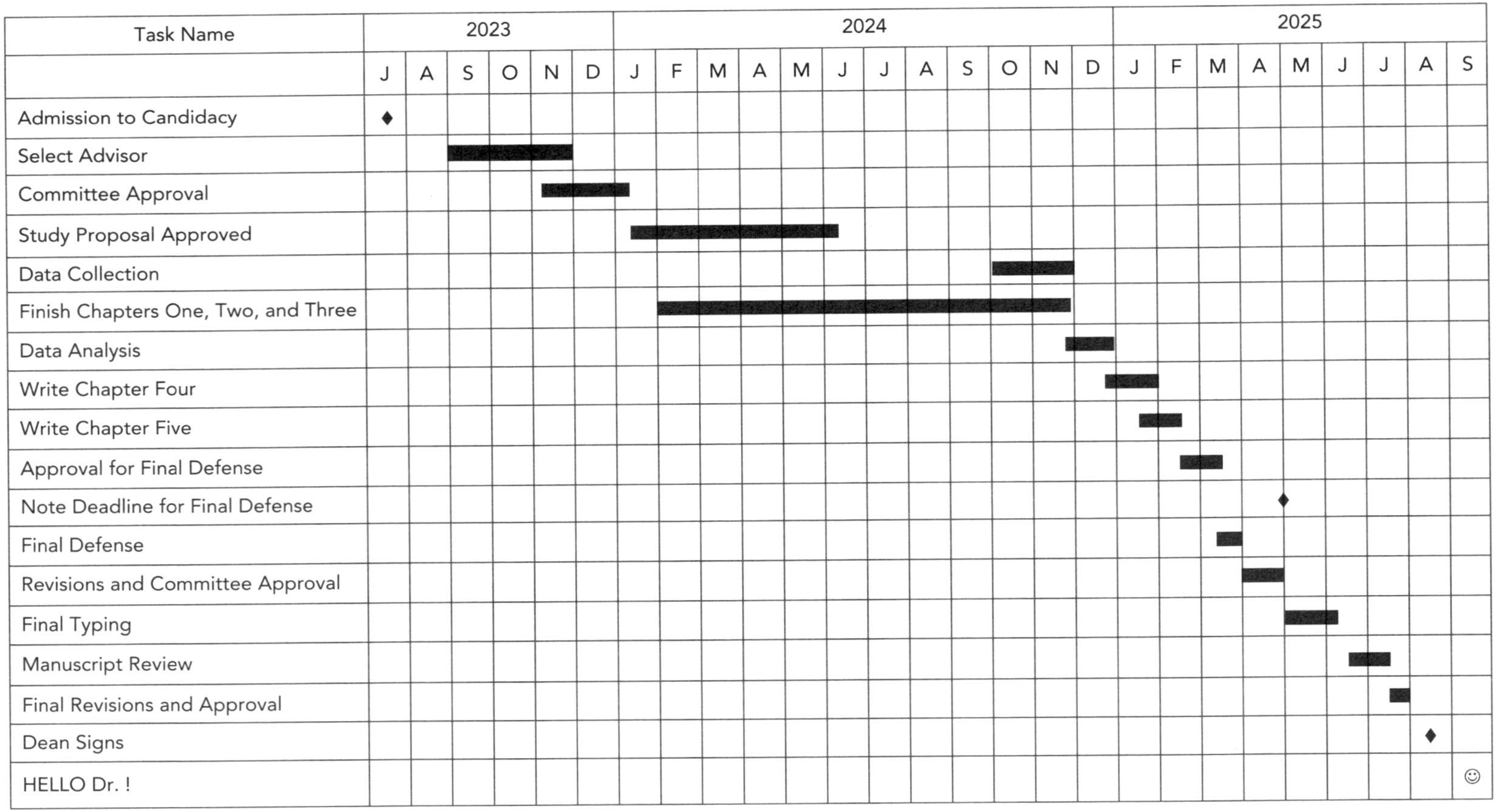

Task Name	2023						2024												2025						
	J	A	S	O	N	D	J	F	M	A	M	J	J	A	S	O	N	D	J	F	M	A	M	J	J	A	S

Following a review of dissertation timetable documents used by various universities, we developed the Dissertation Completion Schedule (DCS). The dissertation student and the advisor cocreate a schedule indicating what is to be completed and when it is to be completed. The DCS is a socially constructed process that encourages dialogue and learning and is intended to serve as a guideline for completion (see Figure 6.2).

Figure 6.2   Dissertation Completion Schedule (DCS)

DATE SCHEDULE INITIATED	
Subject	Dissertation Completion Schedule
Student	
Dissertation Advisor	

Meetings and Communication Expectations

MEETING TYPE	✓	SCHEDULE (DATE, TIME, DURATION, ATTENDEES)
On-site		
Phone		
Text		
Email		
Online		
Social Media		
Other		

Schedule for Completion

OBJECTIVE/ GOAL	DOCUMENT/ DELIVERABLE	DATE DUE	DATE DELIVERED	COMPLETED ✓

Comments:

_____

_____

_____

_____

2. Time Schedule

Creating a strict schedule of an adequate number of hours each day or week to work on your dissertation is essential. We cannot emphasize this enough. No real progress can be made without ongoing involvement with your study. Otherwise, you spin your wheels trying to figure out where you left off the last time. Try to schedule as many unbroken hours as possible for uninterrupted concentration. By scheduling a block of two hours, you can make considerable progress. This follows the recommendation given in *Two Awesome Hours: Science-Based Strategies to Harness Your Best Time and Get Your Most Important Work Done*. Davis (2015), the author, reinforces his recommendations with recent research in neuroscience and psychology. Davis offers five strategies to help carve out "two awesome hours" for peak mental functioning. Davis claims that

> working in tandem with our biology—setting up the conditions for a couple of hours of peak productivity— allows us not only to focus on the tasks that are most important to us and our success but also to restore some sanity and balance to our lives. (p. 15)

Creating two awesome hours for writing your dissertation can make a big difference in the amount of progress you make toward your awesome doctoral degree.

As much as possible, maintain daily progress. This way, your mind stays focused and your subconscious continues working. It helps to set a goal for how much work you will accomplish each day or week and to keep a record to determine whether your goal was met. This keeps you moving and motivated.

REMEMBER

- Plan each day. It's best to block out two hours (or as much time as you can) to work on your dissertation.
- Choose a scheduling strategy that works for you. You may choose to work in terms of hours and minutes worked or pages written. Figure out which works best for you.
- Stick to your schedule.

3. To-Do List

In the time management literature, experts suggest a myriad of techniques for managing a to-do list. Some recommend listing everything that needs to be done and reviewing the list first thing in the morning to confront items that still need to be done. Others recommend keeping a short, doable to-do list. They say you should place only three to six items on your to-do list and make sure you accomplish them. This forces the habit of finishing what you place on your list and results in a feeling of accomplishment.

- One good way to be efficient is to write out a to-do list every day. Separate your to-do list into *A, B,* and *C* priorities. *A* items are your high-priority activities; *B* items may be urgent but not as important; *C* items are those that would be nice to do if you get the time. Start with the *A* items—the ones that must be done. Then move to the *B* items—the ones that probably should be done. *C* items are least important. Don't work on a *C* because it's easy to do. Check off items as you complete them to give yourself a sense of accomplishment. It makes little difference which type of priority technique you use, as long as it works for you. The main thing is to develop the habit of first things first.

- Several time management software programs are available today. A simple approach is to use software programs such as Microsoft Word or Excel to create your task or to-do list. Email programs such as Microsoft Outlook and Gmail also have task lists as standard features and they have the ability to set the task's priority. If you keep your smartphone close by every day, consider using its notes or memo app(s) for easy access. Advantages of using electronic methods include reminders of overdue tasks, the ability to synchronize tasks with phone or email, and the ability to update your to-do list easily. See the resources section at the end of this chapter for some useful software-based approaches to create your to-do list.

- Because everyone plans and works differently, we suggest you research and experiment with different approaches of establishing your to-do lists before deciding on a single system.

HELPFUL HINT

Be sure to keep your to-do list handy on your phone, computer, bulletin board, day planner, bathroom mirror, or in your purse or pocket to enable you to use it regularly.

Working Smart

Working hard is not enough—you need to work smart to ensure that the hours you schedule for dissertation work are truly productive ones. Developing efficient habits and routines and applying the various techniques described in this book are some of the ways you can work with the least amount of wasted time, motion, and money. Here are some recommendations for working smart.

1. Work on Your Dissertation During Times That You Are Most Productive

Are you a night owl?

Are you an early bird?

Pay attention to your biorhythms. Determine the most productive hours for you and try to schedule those hours for dissertation work—your number-one priority. If you're an early bird, consider rising two hours earlier than usual; if you're a night owl, stay up two hours later. Schedule routine tasks for your low-energy periods and your dissertation tasks when you're alert and energetic. It's more productive to work with your daily rhythms and ride your energy peaks.

2. Learn to Say No

Learn to say no to nonvital, trivial requests. In the book, *Secrets for a Successful Dissertation* (Fitzpatrick et al., 1998), the authors expressed this idea well:

> Are you able to say no to favors, fun times, fund-raising, chair positions, family reunions, and frolicking in the park on Sunday afternoons? Because if you are ever going to gain control over your days and nights, and manage your time efficiently, the first lesson to learn is to say no. Say it regretfully, say it remorsefully, say it with clenched teeth, or say it with joy—but say it loud and clear. The world is full of

Time Zappers who will steal your time if you allow them, so put all your good deeds on hold and use the word *no* freely. You'll be glad you did. (p. 97)

Practice making responses such as, "I'm sorry, I'm not available that night," "I can't do that task today, but how about next week?" and "How about asking John instead?" Be gracious with people, but be firm with time.

Your dissertation year is not the time to be president or chairperson of anything, take on additional responsibilities, give presentations, or attend conferences. Eliminate unnecessary activities and accept only those obligations you consider absolutely necessary. You must be ruthless with your time and energy. Learn to say no when you should, and learn to say it without guilt.

> Life can get away from us through thousands of little dribs and drabs.
>
> —B. E. Griessman

3. Schedule Frequent "Joy Breaks"

Throughout your working time, stop and do something pleasurable. Stretch, move about, take some deep breaths, play with your dog, make some tea, or take a walk. Activities like attending plays, musical performances, movies, or museums are also important. These activities can keep you from feeling lonely, discouraged, or depressed. Instead, they energize you and keep you focused. Also, the mind is quite remarkable. When allowed to wander, it often comes up with creative ideas and decisions. You must let your body and mind rest to do your best creative work.

4. Know Your Time Wasters

Two useful tasks to maintain maximum efficiency are (1) determine those things that waste your time and (2) work on reducing or eliminating them. Develop a mindset that judges every activity in terms of whether it brings you closer to completing your dissertation. People must learn to respect your time as much as you do. Make a list of five to ten time wasters in your life and then prioritize them in order of importance. Determine what you think might be the cause(s) of each time waster and generate some possible solutions to reduce or eliminate each one.

5. Reward Your Efforts

Behavior persists when it is rewarded, so give yourself rewards along the way. When you meet a deadline, have coffee with a friend, take the dog for a walk, rent a movie, buy yourself ice cream, or do something else that makes you feel good about your accomplishment. Tell yourself you can't do that thing until you accomplish the allotted amount of dissertation work. For some people, delaying rewards can also work. Some people find it useful to say, "If I don't get this done by that date, then I can't do *X*."

Maintain Balance

Finding the right balance between your dissertation and the rest of your life is difficult. All work and no play puts considerable pressure on you. It can affect your health, attitude, and energy level. Most doctoral students we have known report that the first thing that goes is their fitness routine. They also mention the time strain the dissertation causes in family relationships.

Having a life beyond the dissertation is important. To finish, you need to often put the dissertation first. This means putting other life areas on hold from time to time. However, you needn't always give up other important life activities and devote every waking moment to your dissertation. Working all the time will likely lead to burnout.

One way to get a handle on balancing your life while dissertating is to write down all the things most important in your life (health, family, friends, hobbies, fun, etc.). Then you can identify strategies to help keep them in balance.

Strategies for Getting a Life While Dissertating

1. Take Care of Your Body

Because you must be well to do your best work, remember to get plenty of rest and eat nutritious meals. Good nutrition is required in order to maintain balanced blood sugar levels throughout the day. Low blood sugar can leave you feeling listless. Also, there is considerable evidence about the benefits of deep breathing and regular exercise related to promoting your well-being. The extra oxygen sent to the brain provides energy and helps you think more clearly and creatively. It is also considered a stress buster.

Taking care of your body also means getting adequate sleep. Many doctoral students tend to put sleep on the back burner to get more work done. However, sacrificing a good night's sleep is detrimental to achieving your dissertation goals. Much scientific evidence supports the fact that sleep is critical to health and cognitive functioning and is as important as a healthy diet and regular exercise. Rath (2013), in his book, *Eat Move Sleep: How Small Choices Lead to Big Changes*, cites research studies about the amount of sleep people need to feel fully rested. Researchers state that "95 percent of us need somewhere between seven and nine hours of sleep per night" (p. 161). While it may be tempting to trade sleep for a few extra hours of wakefulness, remember that to get more done, sleep longer. "Sleep is not a luxury. It is a basic necessity" (p. 166).

2. Increase Family Support

To maintain family support, block out hours during the week for family and friends. For example, agree that Saturday nights are available for socializing with friends or that Friday night and Sunday are reserved for family time. Such a plan maintains positive and healthy relationships with the important people in your life. In addition, it cuts down on the guilt that many students feel when these vital relationships are ignored. If you stay true to these time commitments, your friends and family can readily adjust to the schedule.

Another recommendation is to keep your family and friends informed about how you're progressing on the dissertation and even involve them as much as possible. Children love being a part of something so significant in your life. Let them experience your university campus firsthand and include them in all celebratory activities.

Effectively organizing is critical to your success in the dissertation journey. It takes time to learn to be efficient with your time, but it's well worth the effort. We hope you try some of these techniques.

> Physical fitness is the basis for all other forms of excellence.
>
> —John F. Kennedy

SUMMARY

Make organization and planning a top priority in your dissertation journey. It is important to organize your workspace so you can concentrate and be productive. It is equally important to organize your time to maximize energy and keep on track. Create at least three scheduling plans: (1) an overall dissertation timeline, (2) a daily or weekly schedule, and (3) a to-do list. Work smart by developing efficient habits and routines such as (a) working at a time when you are most productive, (b) learning to say no, (c) scheduling frequent "joy breaks," (d) knowing your time wasters, and (e) rewarding your efforts. Maintain balance between your dissertation and the rest of your life by taking care of your body and increasing family support.

Following the guidelines and recommendations presented thus far puts you firmly on the path up the mountain and ready to begin the climb to base camp. The next chapter focuses on the writing phase. It offers you

(Continued)

(Continued)

some important guidelines for attaining a strong, vigorous, and scholarly writing style.

RESOURCES

Dictionary.com

- https://www.dictionary.com/

Evernote

- https://evernote.com/

Microsoft Excel

- https://www.microsoft.com/en-us/microsoft-365/excel

Smartsheet, "How to Create a Simple Gantt Chart in Any Version of Excel" by Diana Ramos

- https://www.smartsheet.com/blog/gantt-chart-excel

Lino Sticky and Photo Sharing

- http://en.linoit.com/

MindTools

- https://www.mindtools.com/

MindTools, "Gantt Charts" by the Mind Tools Content Team

- https://www.mindtools.com/pages/article/newPPM_03.htm

Padlet

- https://padlet.com/

Time, "6 Breathing Exercises to Relax in 10 Minutes or Less" by Jordan Shakeshaft

- https://healthland.time.com/2012/10/08/6-breathing-exercises-to-relax-in-10-minutes-or-less/

Todoist

- https://todoist.com/

Toodledo

- https://www.toodledo.com/

Tom's Planner

- https://www.tomsplanner.com/

Mastering the Academic Style 7

Anyone who wishes to become a good writer should endeavor, before he allows himself to be tempted by the more showy qualities, to be direct, simple, brief, vigorous, and lucid.

—Henry Fowler and Francis Fowler

Qualities of Scholarly Writing

The qualities espoused by Fowler and Fowler in the opening quote represent the heart and soul of good expository writing. However, two additional qualities define the scholarly academic writing required for dissertation writing: *precision* and *logic*. Knowing how to express your ideas in logical sequence and in a clear and concise manner is critical to your success as a scholarly writer. The qualities of logic, precision, clarity, directness, and brevity are also qualities of effective thinking. Zinsser (1994) stated, "Writing is thinking on paper. . . . If you can think clearly about the things you know and care about, you can write—with confidence and enjoyment" (p. vii).

Most dissertation advisors would affirm that scholarly writing is impossible without clear, logical, and precise thinking. There is a close and reciprocal relationship between good writing and clear thinking. Since writing is a reflection of thinking, the quality of your writing depends on how well you think. Clear, logical thinking usually precedes writing; however, the act of writing clarifies your thinking and develops logical thought. This is why many dissertation advisors, rather than endlessly discussing your dissertation, say, "Put it in writing and then we can discuss it."

To express yourself clearly, logically, and with precision, you must be in command of basic writing skills such as constructing grammatical sentences, using appropriate transitions, and remaining focused and concise. If you have difficulty expressing yourself clearly, we strongly suggest that you hire an editor early on to assist you with the writing process. Your committee should not have to spend its time editing or teaching you basic composition skills.

Even if you write reasonably well, you may, like most students, initially experience difficulty writing in the scholarly academic style required for dissertations. This can be verified by many dissertation advisors who received drafts of dissertation chapters that could be classified as clumsy, muddled, and verbose. Reading such writing is tortuous and dulls the senses. The better you write, the fewer revisions you will make and the sooner you will obtain those signatures required for graduation.

The good news is that this kind of writing can be learned. You don't need inspiration—just a good dose of determination, perseverance, and patience. These three characteristics usually can overcome any lack of innate talent or experience writing in a scholarly style. There are many excellent books with good advice on improving your writing. However, the best way to learn to write more effectively is to write a lot, obtain feedback on your writing, and rewrite.

For most people, writing is a difficult, complex, and laborious task requiring self-discipline and mental concentration to stay the course for any length of time. As a doctoral student, you have the extra burden of knowing that your document will be open to public scrutiny and judgment, first to your committee and then to the academic community at large. Your reputation as a scholar, that of your committee, and that of your university are at stake when your dissertation is signed and printed.

This chapter presents guidelines and tips to help you understand some of the critical elements that contribute to scholarly writing. It incorporates key thoughts on writing from a variety of noted authorities, plus our own experiences guiding students in writing academic papers and dissertations.

This book cannot begin to cover the myriad of topics devoted to improving the writing process. Instead, we focus on our observations and those of our colleagues as to the major writing errors made by doctoral students.

Common Writing Problems

We asked a group of dissertation advisors to respond to the question, "What are the most common writing problems you see while guiding dissertation students?" Their responses revolved around four major areas: organization, paragraphs, sentence construction, and direct quotations. The following list summarizes their responses.

> What is written without effort is, in general, read without pleasure.
>
> —Samuel Johnson

- Organization
  - Failure to develop ideas in a logical sequence
  - Lack of organization
  - Lack of consistency
  - Failure to use headings
  - Inappropriate use of the required style manual
  - Little evidence of proofreading and editing
- Paragraphs
  - Paragraphs not developed with a clear center of thought
  - Lack of transitions
  - Introducing a topic and then failing to discuss the topic
  - Lack of details that are explicit and related to the main idea
  - Paragraphs that lack focus
- Sentence Construction
  - Overlong sentences
  - Subject–verb agreement (e.g., *data were* is correct, not *data was*)
- Direct Quotations
  - Inappropriate use of direct quotations
  - Excessive quoting

These specific writing problems relate to the underlying structure of scholarly, academic writing: clarity, conciseness, and coherence. The following section presents some guidelines to help you understand and master these three critical elements that contribute to your success in scholarly writing.

Guidelines for Successful Academic Writing

If you can write clear and concise sentences, you have achieved a good deal and much more if you can assemble them into flowing coherent passages.

—Joseph M. Williams

Clarity

You write clearly when the meaning of your communication is perfectly clear even to those who lack knowledge in your particular field of study. Writing naturally and avoiding verbosity and wordiness are a must; use no more words than are necessary to get your point across. Also, it's easy for readers to become hopelessly mired in a sentence if your construction is too elaborate or ambiguous. Long, complex sentences filled with convoluted phrases and multiple clauses are obstacles to easy reading. Trying to decipher such writing drains your readers' energy and interest.

Guideline 1: Write in a Natural, Unpretentious Style

> The most valuable of all talents is that of never using two words when one will do.
>
> —Thomas Jefferson

Do your best to write naturally, as if you were conversing with an intelligent person unfamiliar with your topic. When you do this, your writing takes on the energy and liveliness of good conversation. So often, students believe they must write in a formal, stilted, grandiose manner. There is artificiality about this kind of writing that makes it boring and tedious for readers. People prefer reading simple, understandable writing.

Guideline 2: Simplify Your Vocabulary

Academic writers tend to use technical terms with abandon. They assume readers understand their specialized language. *Resist jargon— it excludes and mystifies.* If you must use a special term, explain it at the outset. Also remember to choose short words over long ones, especially if they have the same meaning. "Of the 701 words in Lincoln's Second Inaugural Address, a marvel of economy itself, 505 are words of one syllable and 122 are words of two syllables" (Zinsser, 1994, p. 112).

The secret of good writing is to strip every sentence to its cleanest components. Every word that serves no function, every long word that could be a short word, every adverb that carries the same meaning that's already in the verb, every passive construction that leaves the reader unsure of who is doing what—these are the thousand and one adulterants that weaken the strength of a sentence. And they usually occur in proportion to education and rank.

—Zinsser (1994, p. 7)

Guideline 3: Blend Use of Active and Passive Voice

As a scholarly writer, you have the choice of writing sentences in one of two voices—active or passive. The *active voice* is direct, clear, and concise and is used when the subject of the sentence performs the action. In contrast, the *passive voice* is indirect and can be weak, awkward, and wordy. It is used when the subject of the sentence receives the action. Although many scholarly writers today favor active voice, both voices are useful and appropriate. Note that the grammar checker on your word processing program highlights passive constructions, which enables you to decide which choice is most appropriate, given the purpose of your sentence. The following examples contrast the passive and active voices:

Passive: The behavior of two groups of children was compared (by the researchers).

Active: The researchers compared the behavior of two groups of children.

Passive: The advisor was hesitant to approve the research design.

Active: The advisor hesitated to approve the design.

Passive: The dissertation will be edited by members of the committee.

Active: The committee will edit the dissertation.

In the active voice examples above, it is clear who is performing the action. Note that the passive sentences are indirect, wordy, and not always clear about who is responsible for the action. In the passive example, "Research has been conducted to validate this theory," one would wonder who did the research? You? Your professor? Another author?

One sign of the passive voice is the use of linking verbs such as *was, will be, have been,* and *is.* Sentences containing any form of the verb *to be* are eligible for rewriting in active voice. Circle all the linking verbs in your own writing or have a computer highlight them. You will find that 75 percent of them can be eliminated. Write as straightforwardly as you can, using strong verbs—not ones that lack action (*is, was,* etc.).

How do you know if you've used too many passive constructions? On your document, circle or make note of every form of the verb *be* (*am, is, are, had, has, was, were, been,* etc.). Passive voice constructions always include some form of *to be.* If your page is covered with circles, rewrite the page using active verbs.

Both active voice and passive voice have advantages. The active voice reduces wordiness and makes your writing strong and interesting. The passive voice is more formal and impersonal, makes your text wordy, and is often unclear in meaning. However, it is often more readily accepted in scientific writing because you can write without using personal pronouns or names of specific researchers. It represents the conventional means of impersonal reporting and gives an air of objectivity (for example, "Experiments have been conducted to test the hypothesis"). In dissertation writing, the active voice is especially useful in the introduction and discussion chapters as you discuss previous research and then introduce your own. On the other hand, the passive voice is appropriate in the methods chapter, where the steps taken are more important than the doer.

The choice between using the active or passive voice in writing is a matter of style, not correctness. There is nothing inherently wrong with the passive voice, but if you can say the same thing in the active mode, do so. Active verbs give vitality to your writing—it's more direct and vigorous.

In the past, formal writing in the sciences mandated passive voice to create a more objective tone; however, today, major scientific journals and style manuals support the active over the passive voice. Below is a small sampling:

- *The Publication Manual of the American Psychological Association* (APA, 2020) notes that voice is important as it refers to the association between the verb used and its relationship to the object and subject. To create clarity in writing, use the active voice when possible.

- Rather than a passive voice, it is more desirable to use first-person active voice to improve understanding (Oxford Academic, 2018).

- Journals associated with a variety of fields, including science and nature, prefer that authors write directly and use an active voice in order to improve meaning and not confound the reader (Springer Nature, 2018).

While it is necessary to balance the use of passive and active voice contextually and for sentence variety, situations requiring use of passive voice occur infrequently. If your writing does not require these special situations, then reduce the unnecessary passive voice sentences that make your writing tedious and hard to understand. For vigorous, clear writing, choose active voice.

Conciseness

Conciseness refers to writing that is brief and to the point. Much of the academic writing we observe suffers from wordiness—using more words than necessary. With excess verbiage, meaning is lost and readers may become confused. Concise, to-the-point writing is free of redundancy and uses powerful words.

> The ability to simplify means to eliminate the unnecessary so that the necessary may speak.
>
> —Hans Hofmann

Guideline 4: Optimize Sentence Length

Your writing should have a mix of short, medium, and long sentences to keep your readers' interest and to help them understand connections between your various points. Short, choppy sentences affect flow and can't hold complex ideas. On the other hand, long, convoluted sentences can be hard to understand. Your readers' short-term memory can't retain all the words, often causing them to go back to the beginning of the sentence and start again. It's essential not to overwhelm your readers with too much information in each sentence. The following are some suggestions for breaking up long sentences so your readers don't get lost:

- Break long sentences into smaller sentences using transitions such as *first, second, third*, and so on.

- Break up long sentences with internal numbering, such as (1), (2), (3), and so on.

- Break up long sentences with bullet points.

Remember, each sentence should contain *one thought and one thought only.* When sentences have multiple ideas, readers have to figure out the relationship between the ideas, which hampers clear understanding of the text.

Guideline 5: Trim Excess Words

Wordiness will put off most readers. Say what you need to say in as few words as possible, using the simplest language. Strunk and White (1979) stated this idea clearly:

> Vigorous writing is concise. A sentence should contain no unnecessary words, a paragraph no unnecessary sentences, for the same reason that a drawing should have no unnecessary lines and a machine no unnecessary parts. This requires not that the writer make all his sentences short, or that he avoid all detail and treat his subjects only in outline, but that every word tell. (p. 23)

Here are some commonly used phrases that violate conciseness, along with some briefer options:

- *as a matter of fact—in fact*
- *he is a man who—he*
- *in the near future—shortly, soon*
- *this is a subject that—this subject*
- *owing to the fact that—since*

Preposition Alert! Another example of verbosity includes the overuse of prepositions (e.g., *by, under, because, of, for, with*). Good writing is clear, concise, and interesting. Overusing prepositions creates the opposite of that; it causes wordy writing that is boring and hard to understand. It's so much easier to drop in preposition after preposition than to find active verbs that keep your writing powerful and interesting. Preposition overuse is a common writing fault that can be easily corrected. One way to help overcome this habit is to circle or highlight all the prepositions in a sample page of your writing. If you consistently find more than four in a sentence, you need to revise and shorten. *Of* seems to be the worst offender. Trim excess words in your writing by eliminating the overuse of prepositions and their wordy baggage.

Additional culprits to avoid are the compound prepositional phrase and verbs with prepositions. Following is a list of common compound prepositional phrases and verbs with prepositions and their more concise counterparts:

1. COMPOUND PREPOSITIONAL PHRASE	WRITE
with reference to, with regard to, with respect to	about, concerning
by reason of	because
during the course of	during
in close proximity to	near
in order to	to
2. VERBS WITH PREPOSITIONS	WRITE
make an examination of	examine
perform an analysis of	analyze
make assumptions about	assume
give consideration to	consider
is dependent on	depends on

Qualifiers It is also important to trim little qualifiers from your writing. Words that say how you feel and think dilute the forcefulness and persuasiveness of your writing. Examples of such qualifiers are *sort of*, *kind of*, *quite*, *very*, *too*, and *a little*.

Coherence

Coherence in writing refers to the logical, clear, and orderly links between the words, sentences, and paragraphs of your text. It is the quality of order and flow. The term comes from the Latin verb *co-haerere*, meaning *to stick together*. In a coherent academic text, sentences hold together; that is, the movement from one sentence to the next must be logical and smooth—no sudden jumps. In a paragraph, ideas flow smoothly from one sentence to the next, maximizing your readers' understanding of the ideas you wish to convey.

Coherence can be achieved through organizational structure (the order in which ideas are presented), paragraph unity (structuring paragraphs so that each has only one main idea), and sentence cohesion (linking one sentence to the next sentence in a paragraph). Williams (2003) expresses this point elegantly:

> One sentence is cohesive with the next when we see at the beginning of a second sentence information that appeared toward the end of the previous one. That's what creates our experience of "flow." (p. 80)

Guideline 6: Write Clear, Well-Constructed Paragraphs

A well-constructed paragraph organizes your thoughts coherently. Create paragraphs that contain only one main idea. Usually, the main idea is expressed as a topic sentence at the beginning of the paragraph. It is helpful to begin each paragraph with a topic sentence, followed by supporting sentences that illustrate, explain, or clarify your main point. Supporting information might include a specific fact, statistic, direct quotation, anecdote, and so on. Be sure not to write extra-long paragraphs, because they are overwhelming to readers. Also, don't write single sentences as paragraphs. To develop effective, powerful paragraphs, be sure to include these four elements: unity, a topic sentence, coherence, and adequate development.

- *Unity*: a single focus or main idea
- *A topic sentence*: states the central idea of the paragraph. In academic writing, it usually works best at the beginning of a paragraph.
- *Coherence*: clearly connected sentences arranged logically. Each sentence flows smoothly into the next.
- *Adequate development*: sentences support and expand the topic sentence (e.g., use examples and illustrations, cite facts and statistics, use quotes and paraphrases, etc.)

Remember to pay particular attention to the last sentence of each paragraph; it's the critical springboard to the following paragraph. Flow of ideas is an important aspect of writing. Transitions in sentences and paragraphs help maintain flow.

Guideline 7: Use Transitional Words and Phrases

Transitions build bridges between your ideas and help you achieve a coherent document. They act as road signs that guide your readers from one idea to the next. Transitions help make your discussion easy to follow. Readers must understand how the topics relate to one another. Every sentence should be a logical sequel to the one that preceded it. You signal the relationships between sentences and paragraphs with the following sampling of transitional words and phrases.

Frequently Used Transitions	
TO SIGNAL	**EXAMPLES**
Contrast	*but, whereas, yet, still, however, nevertheless, despite, on the contrary, although, on the other hand, conversely*
Addition	*furthermore, subsequently, besides, next, moreover, also, similarly, too, second*
Example	*for instance, an illustration, thus, such as, that is, specifically*
Time or place	*afterward, earlier, at the same time, subsequently, later, simultaneously, above, below, further on, so far, until now*
Conclusion	*therefore, in short, thus, then, in other words, in conclusion, consequently, as a result, accordingly, finally*
Sequence	*then, first, second, third, next*

Other Distinguishing Characteristics of the Academic Style

Formality

Although the definition of *formal* varies among academic disciplines, most fields agree that many words and phrases considered acceptable in conversations are inappropriate in dissertation writing. The following word choices and usage should be avoided.

- colloquialisms: popular words and expressions used in everyday language, such as *part and parcel, pay lip service to,* or *easier said than done*

- slang: expressions peculiar to a particular group, such as *cops, cool,* and so on

- jargon: specialized insider terminology of a specific subgroup of people that may be difficult for others to understand

- contractions: for instance, *won't, they're,* and so on

- clichés: overused expressions such as *think outside the box, at the end of the day,* or *clear as mud.* They betray a lack of original thought.

- platitudes: trite, meaningless statements people use when trying to be helpful, such as *it is what it is, time heals all wounds,* or *it's not rocket science*

Objectivity

Remaining objective in your writing is vital to being perceived as a credible scholar. One way to demonstrate objectivity is to refrain from using biased or discriminatory language. This issue was discussed previously on page 46 of this book; additionally, the APA (2020) style manual provides an in-depth discussion.

A second way to show objectivity in scholarly writing is by using the third-person pronoun. If you desire to make reference to yourself, you could say *the author.* Also refrain from using *you* or *we.* It is important to note, however, that the use of first-person pronouns is acceptable in some genres of research.

Rationality

Rationality in academic writing refers to keeping your language "neutral, impersonal, and reasonable" (Singh & Lukkarila, 2017, p. 101). Adopting this attitude will help convince readers that your assertions are logical and unbiased. In other words, refrain from offering opinion statements or using moralistic, emotional, judgmental, or exaggerated language (hyperbole). Avoid phrases such as *It is right, I believe,* or *I feel.* Also, words or phrases such as *must, always/never, the best, extremely, very,* or that end with *–est* are inappropriate in scholarly writing and may be inaccurate when asserting a claim. Academic audiences are usually suspicious of superlative assertions. Exaggerated words and phrases may also reveal your own biases rather than state a fact. In dissertations, there are only certain sections where it is appropriate to express your opinion.

A technique that experienced academic writers use to express a rational tone is called *hedging*—couching your assertions in cautious or tentative language. It's a way of distinguishing between facts/claims and assertions. As explained by Singh and Lukkarila (2017), "*Hedges* are words or expressions that show hesitation, uncertainty or doubt to any degree on the part of the writer with respect to their claims" (p. 103). For example, you might say *Research suggests* or *It seems likely that* or *It seems reasonable to conclude that.* Using hedges is a way of being more precise in reporting results. Other hedging words include *possibly, perhaps, might, tend, some,* and so on. To expand your hedging vocabulary, Google *hedging words* or *hedging and academic writing.*

Use of Quotations

Academic writing requires the ability to appropriately assimilate the works of others and give proper acknowledgment. When using external sources, you need to consider whether the author's exact words (a direct quote) or the author's ideas (a paraphrase) are the most appropriate way to integrate sources. *Paraphrasing* involves restating an author's words into your own words. *Quoting* involves using another's exact words. Overquoting is a common mistake. Students often string together a series of quotations connected by words such as *similarly, likewise,* and *on the other hand.* Overuse of direct quotes may demonstrate your lack of understanding of the author's ideas and overshadow your own voice. Quotations should be used sparingly.

It is important that you take control of interpreting the work of others. Excessive quoting is a form of laziness on your part. In doing so, you abdicate responsibility for being selective and doing your own interpretation for the reader.

Don't start your sentences with a quotation followed by your own words. Instead, start with your words and support them with quoted or paraphrased material.

Verbs That Introduce

In academic writing, the frequent use of paraphrased or quoted information creates a challenge to find ways to vary the verbs used. However, variety in verb use generates more interesting texts; it avoids repetitive constructions such as *Smith said* or *Smith stated.* These words provide more than variety; they also provide exactness. Consider some of the following instead:

acknowledged	confirmed	implied
addressed	contended	maintained
affirmed	contradicted	negated
agreed	declared	noted
argued	discussed	refuted
asserted	disputed	reported
believed	emphasized	thought
commented	endorsed	wrote

Academic Checklist

Below is an academic writing checklist that encompasses the tips and guidelines presented in this chapter. It will be useful in completing a self-assessment of your own writing as you build toward mastering the academic style. The checklist will also be helpful in obtaining feedback from others.

ACADEMIC WRITING CHECKLIST

CLARITY

_____Used a natural and unpretentious style

_____Defined terms where needed

_____Information presented precisely and accurately

_____Used a blend of active and passive voice

CONCISENESS

_____Used a mixture of short, medium, and long sentences

_____Trimmed excess and redundant words and phrases

_____Avoided overuse of prepositions

_____Trimmed qualifiers (e.g., *very, too, a little*)

COHERENCE

_____Wrote well-constructed paragraphs that contained one main idea

_____Included a topic sentence for each paragraph

_____Included adequate detail that supported and expanded the topic sentence

_____Wrote sentences that were clearly connected and arranged logically

_____Used transitional words and phrases

FORMALITY

_____Avoided unnecessary jargon, colloquialisms, and slang

_____Avoided contractions

_____Avoided clichés and platitudes

OBJECTIVITY

_____Avoided bias or discriminatory language

_____Used the third-person pronoun (except when appropriate)

_____Avoided using *you* or *we*

RATIONALITY

_____Used language that was neutral, impersonal, and reasonable

_____Refrained from offering opinion statements

_____Avoided moralistic, emotional, judgmental, or exaggerated language

_____Used hedging techniques to couch assertions

QUOTATIONS

_____Used an appropriate combination of paraphrasing and quoting

_____Avoided overquoting

_____Avoided starting sentences with a quote

_____Used a variety of verbs when paraphrasing or quoting

SUMMARY

Scholarly academic writing requires the ability to express your ideas logically, clearly, concisely, and with precision. Such writing requires command of basic writing skills, such as logical organization, good sentence and paragraph construction, and appropriate transitions. This chapter offered seven guidelines to help you understand and master the three critical elements that contribute to scholarly academic writing: clarity, conciseness, and coherence. In addition, other distinguishing characteristics of the academic style were discussed: formality, objectivity, rationality, and use of quotations. Additionally, attention was given to verbs that introduce paraphrased or quoted information. Using different verbs provides not only variety but exactness.

RESOURCES

Scribbr, English Mistakes Commonly Made in a Dissertation: Example

* https://www.scribbr.com/language-rules/common-mistakes/

(Continued)

(Continued)

Academic Writing in English, Common Problems and How to Avoid Them

- https://www.awelu.lu.se/language/common-problems-and-how-to-avoid-them/

Purdue University, Online Writing Lab (OWL)

- https://owl.purdue.edu/

Grammarly

- https://app.grammarly.com/

Daily Page

- https://www.dailypage.co/

PART III

Next Objective: Base Camp

Source: https://istockphoto.com/sihasakprachum

To climb a mountain, one must start at the base.

—Chinese saying

Writing the Introduction 8

The introduction chapter of your dissertation sets the stage for your study and typically consists of the following sections: an introduction to the study, the research problem, the theoretical or conceptual framework, the purpose statement, a statement about the type of research method and questions/hypotheses, the significance of the study, the delimitations, the assumptions, a definition of terms, an organization of the remaining chapters, and a summary that states the key points made in the chapter. Most introductions in the social sciences follow a similar pattern; however, they may vary according to the type of research methodology used.

The overall structure of the introduction chapter moves from the general to the specific, beginning with an overview of the general area under study and ending with specific research questions/hypotheses. Think of writing this chapter in a *V* or funnel-shaped fashion, as shown in Figure 8.1.

To help you focus your introduction, first draw a large funnel and fill it in to help you visually focus your topic. The top of the funnel begins with an introduction, a description of the general area to be studied. Next, identify a more specific problem within the general area. Say why this problem is important to study and specify what is already known about the problem. Then, specify what is not known about the problem that is important to study. Finally, state a specific purpose statement in one or two sentences, followed by research questions that guide the study.

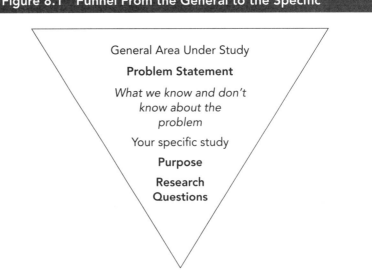

Figure 8.1   Funnel From the General to the Specific

The Introductory Paragraph

A good introduction states the focus of your study and discusses the general issues that surround it. It describes the broad, general context and pertinent background information related to the problem you investigated. Your introduction includes a brief summary of literature and research about the problem you investigated, leading to a description of the problem statement. In other words, what is the current understanding of your topic? Don't include a complete history of your study area.

The opening sentences of your introduction should grab the readers' attention and draw them into the study. Creswell (2015) calls the first sentence a *narrative hook*. A good narrative hook does the following: "cause the reader to pay attention, elicit emotional or attitudinal responses, spark interest, and encourage the reader to continue reading" (p. 65). Some examples of narrative hooks might include interesting statistical data, a stimulating question, or a relevant quotation. Generally, the introduction consists of about three to five pages; however, it may vary, depending on the nature of the study and the preferences of your advisor.

> ## NOTE
>
> Because the primary function of the introductory chapter is to set the context of your study, be cautious about using an overabundance of citations. The information provided in the introduction expands to include a detailed, comprehensive review of related literature.

Problem Statement

Once you introduce your topic area, you then narrow it to a specific research problem that contributes to knowledge and practice. You can show this contribution in several ways: filling a gap in the research or literature, exploring an unanswered question, extending previous research, resolving contradictory findings, or "giving voice to people silenced, not heard, or rejected in society" (Creswell, 2015, p. 63). In this section, you must provide sufficient evidence to support the extent of the problem and to convince the reader the problem is real, important, and timely.

A *research problem* can be defined as

> the issue that exists in the literature, in theory, or in practice that leads to a need for the study. The research problem in a study becomes clear when the researcher asks, "What is the need for this study?" or "What problem influenced the need to undertake this study?" (Creswell, 2002, p. 80)

The problem statement tells the story behind the variables or concepts to be studied and provides background for the purpose statement and research questions.

The problem statement should do the following:

- Have a line of logic that leads the reader to the purpose statement
- Provide a background to the variables or concepts to be studied
- Cite literature sources, but not extensively
- Conclude with the "need to know"—formally stated as *significance of the study*

Line of Logic

The problem statement begins with a general introduction to the study and, through a careful line of reasoning, focuses down to become more detailed and specific to your study. Your writing should be clear, precise, and directional. There should be a sequential line of logic. For example, the research problem leads directly to the purpose statement, which leads directly to the research questions. An important point to remember is that the line of logic comes from you. It cannot be found directly in the literature.

Background to the Problem's Variables or Concepts

Providing background information to your research problem requires answering the following questions:

1. What do we already know about this problem?

2. What do we *not* know about this problem? What has not been answered adequately in previous research and practice?

3. What do we want to know about this problem?

The problem statement is the discrepancy between what we already know and what we want to know. It is necessary to provide background information about both what is known and what is not known. The problem statement also tells the story about why we care—why we should conduct this study. It is important for the reader to know what is unique and different from previous research. Try to conceive of your study as a large jigsaw puzzle with a piece missing. Or you may conceive of your study as fulfilling an indicated need for further advancement of previous research. That missing piece is the gap you want to fill. To discover that missing piece, you must read widely in the literature base of your topic area.

When all of these studies are aggregated, you can then tell something about the problem's domain. (See Figure 8.2.)

Literature Sources

The variables or factors you selected for study must exist within some conceptual or theoretical framework that you develop from reading the literature. You cannot pull your topic out of a hat. Appropriate citations from the literature help provide a justification for selecting these variables or concepts. Creating a conceptual framework is one of the few places where you have the opportunity to display original thought. If, however, you conduct an inductive qualitative study, your variables or

Figure 8.2   Defining the Problem's Domain

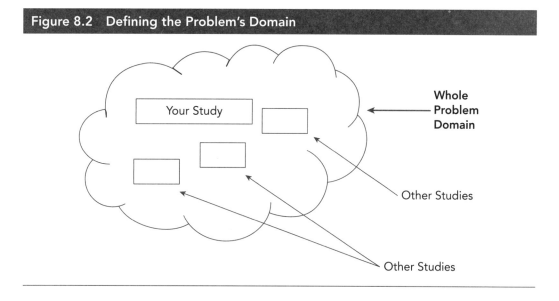

concepts emerge from the data. Rather than starting with a conceptual framework, you investigate broad, general areas that become more focused through data gathering in the field.

Citing the literature helps you build a case for why your research should be undertaken. The references and quotations support your arguments. However, keep in mind that in most cases, citations should be used sparingly in the problem statement. It is not a formal review of the literature.

For impact, keep your sentences short and write an opening sentence that stimulates interest. In short, your introductory chapter should convince your readers of the study's need and value.

Need to Know

What is the need for this particular study? Why does this specific study need to be conducted? So what? What contribution will your study make to the literature or to the field? Who benefits from your study and in what way? The major discussion of the study's importance may be found in the significance of the study section.

Common Errors in Writing the Problem Statement

Here are some common errors students make in submitting drafts of their problem statements:

- Failing to get to the point. Avoid tedious length in introducing the study. The reader wants to know what your study is about.

- Making the reader believe that we already know the answer. If we know it, then we don't need to study it.

- Covering extraneous issues, whether interesting or not. These are "rabbit runs"—interesting but irrelevant to the topic. Resist the temptation to share with the reader the volume of interesting but irrelevant information you accumulated.

- Being inconsistent. The problem should be clearly and logically related to the purpose statement and research questions.

- Stating what we should *do* rather than what we want to *know*. Such phrases as *we must, we should*, and *it is imperative that* belong in a position paper. In short, stay off a soapbox.

- Writing in "dissertationese" rather than in English. This causes your writing to be stilted, awkward, and artificial. Just say what you mean in natural phrases.

- Using unnecessary technical language and jargon. This keeps the reader from understanding the main idea of what you're trying to say.

- Using extensive quotations and references. These get in the way of the logical flow of ideas.

- Using abstruse arguments. Refrain from making points that are unclear or difficult to understand. Write in a clear, simple, and straightforward manner.

- Engaging in personal reflections or editorializing. Reserve this for Chapter 5 (the summary, conclusions, and recommendations of the study).

- Making unsupported claims or statements. The problem must be written in the context of theory and relevant literature.

- Using disjointed recitation of the studies cited. You create the line of logic and use literature citations to substantiate your points.

The opening sentences of your dissertation should be approached thoughtfully and carefully, for this is the place to win or lose your audience. Therefore, introduce your topic in a way that engages readers—that captures their interest and makes them want to continue reading. Creswell (2004) called these opening lines the *narrative hook*, a term he claimed is "drawn from English composition, meaning words that serve to draw, engage, or hook the reader into the study" (p. 102). A convincing narrative hook, according to Creswell (2015), might include one or more of the following:

1. Statistical data (e.g., "More than 50 percent of the adult population experiences depression today.")

2. A provocative question (e.g., "Why are school policies that ban smoking in high schools not being enforced?")

3. A clear need for research (e.g., "School suspension is drawing increased attention among scholars in teacher education.")

4. The intent or purpose of the study (e.g., "The intent of this study is to examine how clients construe the therapist–client relationship.") (p. 65)

There are a variety of other possibilities for introducing your study; the main thing to remember is to begin in an engaging manner that will interest your audience so they keep on reading.

Theoretical or Conceptual Framework

Doctoral students hate to hear these words from their dissertation advisor: "Your study sounds promising, but what is your theoretical framework?" This question is often met with silence, raised eyebrows, or shrugged shoulders, indicating more information is needed about this term. In discussing the theoretical framework, Merriam (2001) stated,

> A colleague of mine once commented that if she could have figured out what a theoretical framework was early on, she could have cut a year off of her graduate studies! Indeed, the theoretical or conceptual framework of a study and where theory fits into a research study continues to mystify and frustrate many a novice (and sometimes experienced) researcher. (pp. 44–45)

Few texts or books about writing a dissertation or thesis discuss the process, importance, or purpose of developing a conceptual or theoretical framework and making it explicit. It is often the missing link in student scholarship. Hopefully, this section will ground your understanding in this important aspect of designing and clarifying your research.

What Is a Conceptual or Theoretical Framework?

It is a lens through which your research problem is viewed. It can be a theory, a construct that conceptualizes your study's focus, or a research perspective. Miles and Huberman (2014) defined it this way: "A conceptual framework explains, either graphically or in narrative form, the main things to be studied—the key factors, variables, or constructs—and the presumed relationships among them" (p. 20). Some of the visual forms a conceptual framework might take include tree diagrams, mind maps, flowcharts, concept maps, or diagrams such as triangles, circles, and so on. In their book, *Qualitative Data Analysis,* Miles and Huberman provide several graphic illustrations followed by descriptive narrative that serve as examples of conceptual or theoretical frameworks.

The conceptual or theoretical framework provides the boundaries or scaffolding for your study. Like a microscope, it narrows your field of vision, thus helping you limit the scope of your study. After all, it is usually not possible to study everything about your research topic. Making your conceptual or theoretical framework explicit provides clarity for the reader as to exactly what your study is about and provides the focus and content for making decisions about your study's design. By not grounding your study within an explicit conceptual or theoretical frame, your study takes on a "So what?" quality.

How Does a Conceptual Framework Differ from a Theoretical Framework?

Often, the terms *conceptual framework* and *theoretical framework* are used interchangeably and rarely is a differentiation made. A *theory* is a discussion about related concepts, assumptions, and generalizations, while *concepts* can be defined as words or phrases that represent several interrelated ideas. If your study is grounded in a particular theory or theories, then perhaps the better term would be *theoretical framework*, since theory would be used to explain the particular phenomenon under study. It implies a higher level of conceptual organization. If your study does not include a specific theory, it still contains concepts and subconcepts that define the interrelationship of the ideas contained in your study. Some studies contain a review of theory as well as a conceptual framework. We recommend a conference with your dissertation advisor to determine the best approach for your particular study. Remember, no study is without some implicit framework. Your challenge is to discover it and make it explicit.

Why Do You Need a Conceptual or Theoretical Framework?

A well-defined conceptual or theoretical framework helps you to view your area of interest more acutely. Similar to a telescope or microscope, a conceptual or theoretical framework narrows and brings into focus your field of vision, which is necessary for limiting the scope of your study. It helps define the research problem and structures the writing of your literature review. In addition, it acts as a filtering tool to select appropriate research questions and to guide data collection, analysis, and interpretation of findings.

How Do You Find a Conceptual or Theoretical Framework?

The best way to select an appropriate conceptual or theoretical framework for your study is to immerse yourself in the research and theoretical literature related to your topic of interest. You may not find a specific theory to guide your study; however, you will discover a variety of interrelated core concepts and subconcepts from which to frame your study.

Example 1 of a Conceptual Framework

The following are sections from a quantitative dissertation about student persistence and academic success in an institution of higher education. The researcher (Spindle, 2006) prepared a separate section in Chapter 1 devoted to the study's underlying theories.

CONCEPTUAL FRAMEWORK

To properly frame this study . . . it was appropriate to go to the recognized experts in college persistence. These theorists studied college persistence for over 35 years and developed models that have been tested and validated.

Student persistence is complex, made up of many variables (Lewallen, 1993). Studies since the 1970s attempted to isolate the most important and influential elements of student retention, attrition, and ultimately persistence to bachelor's degree completion. Two theorists who heavily influenced the direction of this research were Vincent Tinto and Alexander Astin (Blecher, Michael, & Hagedon, 2002; Colbert, 1999; Hutto, 2002).

Vincent Tinto in 1975 developed his "Model of Student Departure," which postulated that students come to a college with a particular background molded by their own unique genetics and environmental experiences and are guided by certain aspirations toward particular goal completions. This background and goal setting impacted the academic

(Continued)

(Continued)

and social integration of the student at the university. Ultimately, Tinto theorized that the successful academic and social integration of a student led to successful persistence to degree completion (Blecher, Michael, & Hagedorn, 2002; Tinto, 1975). Tinto's theory has been widely quoted and reviewed over the last 30 years as evidenced by over 400 citations and at least 170 dissertations focusing on this theory (Braxton, Milem, & Sullivan, 2000). The basic precepts of the theory have been affirmed by many researchers (Aitken, 1982; Benjamin, 1993; Pascarella, 1983; Terenzini, 1977, 1980, 1985).

In 1970, Alexander Astin began with a general education model focusing on how students are impacted by their college experience. He then developed and expanded it over the next few years and referred to it as the "Input–Environment–Output" persistence model (Astin, 1970, 1975). Students enter higher education with unique "input" variables, again based on their own genetics and particular environmental experiences (Astin, 1970). . . . Astin defined the "environment" variables as "those aspects of higher educational institutions that are capable of affecting the student" (Astin, 1970, p. 3). These environmental variables can be anything from institutional policies, associations with other students, support programs, facilities, to specific curriculum (Astin, 1970). . . .

In conjunction with this structure, Astin designed a "Theory of Involvement" and theorized that the level of involvement of a student's interactions within the university environment was a major factor in the eventual persistence of the student (Astin, 1970, 1984). . . . Hutto's literature review on student retention revealed that Astin is considered the foremost researcher on student involvement theory primarily because . . . Astin has led the nation's longest running study of college environments (Astin, 2003).

Both Tinto and Astin use an Input–Environment–Output approach to student persistence. Both acknowledge the role of student biological and environmental independent variables on the dependent outcome variables of persistence and ultimate academic success and the possible mediating role of university environmental variables on the input variables.

Note: The researcher then proceeded to describe the applicability of the Input–Environment–Output Model to his particular study.

Source: Spindle, B. (2006). *A study of Alaska native student persistence and academic success at the University of Alaska Anchorage.* Doctoral Dissertation, University of La Verne, California.

To see additional examples of describing a conceptual or theoretical framework, refer to Creswell's book, *Research Design: Qualitative, Quantitative, and Mixed Methods Approaches* (2002). In this book, Creswell provided models for writing a quantitative theoretical perspective section (see pp. 127–130). He also provided a description and examples of qualitative theory use (see pp. 131–136).

Example 2 of a Conceptual Framework

This example is from a dissertation titled *An Exploratory Study of the Ways in Which Superintendents Use Their Emotional Intelligence to Address Conflict in Their Organizations* (Geery, 1997).

The purpose of this study was to describe the knowledge, skills, behaviors, and strategies associated with emotional intelligence that superintendents perceived they use to address conflict in their organizations. This study also determined the impact emotional intelligence had on superintendents' perceptions of their ability to lead and manage their organizations. (Geery, 1997)

The conceptual framework for this study was the five concept areas of emotional intelligence: understanding their own emotions, managing their own emotions, motivating themselves, recognizing the emotions of others, and handling relationships with others. The matrix that outlines this conceptual framework follows. Notice how this framework mirrors the purpose of the study.

	KNOWLEDGE	SKILLS	BEHAVIORS	STRATEGIES
Understanding their own emotions	Uses emotional self-awareness Uses emotional self-knowledge	Displays self-regard Is intuitive Is insightful Is reflective	Is confident Is assertive	Recognizes one's strengths and weaknesses Capitalizes on strengths and improves weaknesses through self-improvement

(Continued)

(Continued)

	KNOWLEDGE	SKILLS	BEHAVIORS	STRATEGIES
Managing their own emotions	Understands and uses impulse control Understands and uses self-control	Is resilient Is flexible Displays a tolerance for dealing with stress	Holds back negative emotions to remain positive Displays positive emotional behavior	Reframes problems Uses humor Takes time out to relax
Motivating themselves	Understands and believes in one's potential (potency)	Is optimistic Is hopeful Is persistent Approaches challenges with enthusiasm	Delays gratification Displays positive energy Accepts responsibility for own behavior Focuses attention on the task at hand	Sets personal goals Breaks down large tasks into smaller steps Celebrates small successes
Recognizing the emotions of others	Understands and demonstrates empathy	Reads people's nonverbal behavior Listens actively Demonstrates insight about other's feelings, motives, and concerns	Pays attention to people and relationships Mirrors others' movements and tones Demonstrates regard and compassion for others	Develops rapport with colleagues and employees Allows employees to express emotions Provides emotional support for others
Handling relationships with others	Understands how to develop relationships	Influences, persuades, and inspires others Appropriate expression and transfer of emotion Harnesses the willing participation of others	Demonstrates respect for others Recognizes and responds appropriately to people's feelings and concerns Makes personal connections with others Promotes cooperation	Models emotional intelligence Builds trust in relationships Boosts organizational morale Builds collaboration among people Gives praise, recognition, and rewards

Purpose Statement

By the time the reader gets to the purpose statement, there should be no doubt about what you will be doing in your study. The purpose statement, usually written in a single sentence or paragraph, clearly and succinctly states the intent of your study—what exactly you're going to find out. It represents the essence of your study and reflects its parameters. The purpose statement, according to Creswell (2009), "is the most important statement in the entire study, and it needs to be clearly and specifically presented" (p. 111). The purpose is clarified when you specify the variables or concepts under study and indicate whether your study is qualitative or quantitative. In any one study, you may find one or more of these types of measurements.

It is important to realize that purpose statements vary according to specialized research designs. A qualitative purpose statement uses words drawn from that specialized line of inquiry and often reflects the procedures of an emerging design format. Sometimes qualitative researchers use words such as *intent, aim,* or *objective* to draw attention to the study's intent. A quantitative purpose statement should contain the identified variables, the relationship among the variables, the participants, and the site of the research. Examples that illustrate the difference between qualitative, quantitative, and mixed-methods purpose statements can be found in *Research Design: Qualitative, Quantitative, and Mixed Methods Approaches* by Creswell (2009).

REMEMBER

Include the purpose statement and research questions in each chapter. Be sure they appear exactly the same throughout the dissertation. Don't get creative!

Statement About Method Type and Research Questions/Hypotheses

A question well stated is a question half answered.

—Stephen Isaac and William B. Michael

Your topic was introduced, background information provided, and the purpose clearly stated. In this section of the dissertation, you introduce the type of method used and state the research questions or hypotheses for the study. Your research questions/hypotheses guide the study and usually provide the structure for presenting the results of the research. Generally, good research questions should have the following:

• Clear variables/concepts

• Obvious measurement type (description, relationship, difference)

• "Thing words" clarified (*success, processes, achievement, factors,* etc.)

Significance and Relevance

This section is a more detailed explanation of the *why* of your study. Does it explore an important issue, meet a recognized need, or fill in a gap in the knowledge base? You must build an argument for the worth or significance of your research—how it should be useful to knowledge, practitioners, and policy makers.

You have to convince your reader, especially your advisor and committee, of the need for this particular study. To support your argument, you can summarize writings of experts who identified your problem as an important one and urged that research be conducted about it. Second, you can show specific data that indicate the severity of the problem and the need to resolve it.

Delimitations

This section clarifies the boundaries of your study. It is the way to indicate to the reader how you narrowed your study's scope. You control the delimitations—what will be included and what will be left out. The following are some typical delimitations:

• Time of the study (e.g., February 2018 through April 2018)

• Location of the study (e.g., districts in Southern California or urban areas only)

• Sample of the study (e.g., principals and superintendents)

• Selected aspects of the problem

• Selected criteria of the study

The following are some ways to express a dissertation's delimitations:

• Only those districts with student enrollments less than 1,000 were included in this study.

- Those surveyed in this study consisted of female managers in their first supervisory position.

- The study included only those organizations that matched the selection criteria established for the study. The criteria for selection included . . .

Assumptions

Not all studies include assumptions. Whether or not they are indicated depends on the desires of your advisor and committee members. Basically, assumptions are what you take for granted relative to your study. The following are some examples of assumptions:

- The sample studied was representative of the total population of nurses employed at the St. Paul's Memorial Hospital.

- Responses received from the participating managers accurately reflected their professional opinions.

- High school students can remember what their perceptions were of the bilingual program in which they participated 10 to 12 years ago.

- The participants in this study answered all of the interview questions openly and honestly.

Definition of Terms

This section of the dissertation provides the definition for the terms used that do not have a commonly known meaning or that have the possibility of being misunderstood. These terms should be operationally defined—that is, defined according to how the terms are used in your study. You can choose to define them in any way you like in order to clarify what you mean when you use that particular term. Unless they are clearly defined, they can be open to numerous interpretations. For example, the term *achievement* in education can refer to a variety of meanings. One operational definition may be the level of test scores throughout a school, or it could mean skill in playing the piano. It is appropriate to paraphrase or to specifically cite definitions used in the literature. The following are some examples of definitions of terms used in dissertations:

- *Transformational leader*: Someone in authority who articulates a clear vision for the future

- *Empowerment*: A process that enables people to do what they do best and for which they are held accountable
- *Site-based management*: A system that increases people's authority at the school site and involves them in implementing decisions

REMEMBER

Define each new term the first time it appears in the study.

Organization of the Study

Usually, Chapter 1 concludes with a section that delineates the contents of the remaining chapters in the study. Here is an example:

> The remainder of the study is organized into five chapters, a bibliography, and appendixes in the following manner. Chapter 2 presents a review of the related literature dealing with evolving trends in the practices and procedures used to evaluate superintendents. Chapter 3 delineates the research design and methodology of the study. The instrument used to gather the data, the procedures followed, and determination of the sample selected for study are described. An analysis of the data and a discussion of the findings are presented in Chapter 4. Chapter 5 contains the summary, conclusions, and recommendations of the study. The study concludes with a bibliography and appendixes.

SUMMARY

When writing your dissertation's introductory chapter, be sure to include background information to all the variables and concepts directly related to your study, the importance of your study to the field, and an explicit discussion of your study's conceptual or theoretical framework. Write a clear and succinct purpose statement and research questions that clearly define the parameters of your study. It is also important to include a delimitations section that clarifies the scope of your study and a definition of terms section that operationally defines the specific terms used in your study. A concluding statement delineates the contents of the study's remaining chapters. The next chapter helps you acquire the skills to conduct a substantive, comprehensive, and systematic literature review in your field of interest.

RESOURCES

Scribbr, "What Is a Theoretical Framework? Guide to Organizing," by Sara Vinz; revised by Tegan George

- https://www.scribbr.com/research-paper/theoretical-framework/

Stanford University, Statement of Purpose

- https://ed.stanford.edu/sites/default/files/statement-of-purpose_revised_4.pdf

Scribbr, "How to Write a Thesis or Dissertation Introduction," by Tegan George and Shona McCombes

- https://www.scribbr.com/dissertation/introduction-structure/

Purdue University Online Writing Lab, University Thesis and Dissertation Templates

- https://owl.purdue.edu/owl/graduate_writing/thesis_and_dissertation/University_Thesis_and_Dissertation_Templates.html

The Literature Review 9

The greatest gift you can give yourself as a researcher is to read and analyze the literature surrounding your study as early as possible. Too often, students see the literature review as something to do while waiting for their data to be collected. This may be because they don't fully understand the importance and purpose of the review. It may also be because they are uncertain of the exact procedures to follow for conducting a literature search. The importance of a literature search is stated by Hart (2009) in his book, *Doing a Literature Review*:

> A review of the literature is important because without it you will not acquire an understanding of your topic, of what has already been done on it, how it has been researched, and what the key issues are. In your written project you will be expected to show that you understand previous research on your topic. This amounts to showing that you have understood the main theories in the subject area and how they have been applied and developed, as well as the main criticisms that have been made of work on the topic. (p. 1)

A similar notion was advanced by Boote and Beile (2005); they made the following points:

> A substantive, thorough, sophisticated literature review is a precondition for doing substantive, thorough, sophisticated research. . . . A researcher cannot perform significant research

without first understanding the literature in the field. Not understanding the prior research clearly puts a researcher at a disadvantage. (p. 3)

A comprehensive, up-to-date literature review allows you to get to the frontier in your area of research and, at the same time, become an expert in your field. In addition, the insights and knowledge you gain provide the basis for a better-designed study and enhance the possibility of obtaining significant results. A review of the literature is a vital part of the research process.

A literature review is a two-phase activity. In the first phase, you conduct the review by identifying appropriate resources, searching for relevant materials, and analyzing, synthesizing, and organizing the results; the second phase is the actual writing of the review, which culminates in the completed product. The literature review section of a study is found where reference is made to the related research and theory around your topic. The location may vary, depending on your selected methodology. For example, in some qualitative studies, authors might choose to locate the literature section toward the end of the dissertation, following discussion of the emerging theory, which, according to Creswell (2004), "allows the views of the participants to emerge without being constrained by the views of others from the literature" (p. 90). Researchers in quantitative studies typically place their discussion of the literature at the beginning of a study, usually in a separate chapter titled "Review of the Literature." Frequently, the literature is referred to again at the end of the study when comparing the study's findings to the literature.

This chapter helps you acquire the skills to conduct and write a thorough and systematic review of the literature in your field of interest. The chapter includes the purpose and scope of the literature review, notes on its preparation, specific steps in conducting a literature review, and strategies and techniques for writing the literature review.

Purpose and Scope

What is a literature review? According to Creswell (2004), "A literature review is a written summary of journal articles, books, and other documents that describe the past and current state of information; organizes the literature into topics; and documents a need for a proposed study" (p. 89). Reviewing the literature involves locating, analyzing, synthesizing, and organizing previous research and documents (periodicals, books, abstracts, etc.) related to your study area. The goal is to obtain a detailed, cutting-edge knowledge of your particular topic. To do this, you must immerse yourself in your subject by reading extensively and voraciously. A solid and comprehensive review of the literature accomplishes several important purposes. It helps you to do the following:

1. Focus the purpose of your study more precisely.

2. Develop a conceptual or theoretical framework that might be used to guide your research.

3. Identify key variables for study and suggest relationships among them if you are completing a quantitative study; if you are conducting a qualitative study, identify the concepts or topics you plan to study.

4. Provide a historical background for your study.

5. Uncover previous research similar to your own that can be meaningfully extended.

6. Determine the relationship of your topic relative to current and past studies.

7. Identify scholars and theorists in your area of study.

8. Form a basis for determining the significance of your study.

9. Uncover questionnaires or tests previously validated.

10. Link your findings to previous studies. (Do your findings support or contradict them?)

We hope we convinced you of the importance of doing an early and comprehensive review of the literature. The benefits are numerous, especially in the initial stages of designing a dissertation study.

One of the biggest frustrations students encounter is determining how long and how comprehensive the review should be. Even though you must read broadly to develop perspective about your topic, don't make the mistake of thinking that you must include in the bibliography every book, article, or study read. The literature review is not an aggregation of every book and article related to your topic; it is always selective. Therefore, you must be discriminating and include only the most relevant information. Remember that bigger is not better! The shotgun approach indicates a lack of knowledge about what is relevant information. Unfortunately, no magic formula exists to guide your selection; it is a judgment call on your part. You know it is time to quit when you keep encountering the same references and can't find important new resources.

Generally speaking, most advisors prefer the literature review chapter to be around 20 to 40 pages. However, keep in mind that this can vary, depending on the breadth and complexity of your study and the preferences of your advisor. Take time to clarify your advisor's preferences prior to writing the review.

Preparation

Step 1 in writing your literature review requires that you become knowledgeable about what references are available and where to find them, what services your library provides, and the regulations and procedures regarding the use of library materials.

It is also wise to cultivate a friendship with a librarian or two. Their knowledge and expertise can save you considerable time in searching for information. Most librarians are willing to make appointments to help you create a search strategy, determine appropriate print and electronic databases for your research needs, and explain the interlibrary loan services available to you. It is also a good idea to consult librarians about nontraditional sources on your topic, such as think tanks, professional associations, government documents, and publications from nonprofit organizations.

Because the majority of academic literature is now available online, you needn't spend hours using call numbers to browse the stacks of your library. Most of your research will be conducted online using your own computer from home or the office. This means that you must become computer literate and internet savvy to make your dissertation research easier. Becoming familiar with search engines and how they work (using keywords, Boolean operators, truncation, and online help) is essential. There certainly are downsides to computers. Any user knows the frustration of crashes, lost files, and inoperable software. But, for the most part, it will be your best friend and the most essential tool for completing your dissertation. Hardware and software advances continue to make conducting research more and more efficient.

Conducting a thorough and scholarly review of the literature involves eight basic steps. The steps are not necessarily sequential; you will probably move back and forth between them.

1. Identify keywords or descriptors.

2. Create a search query.

3. Identify relevant literature sources.

4. Search the literature and collect relevant materials.

5. Critically read and analyze the literature.

6. Synthesize the literature.

7. Organize the literature.

8. Write the literature review.

Step 1: Identify Keywords or Descriptors

Before beginning a search of the literature, it is important to develop a search strategy that effectively locates useful, relevant information. This involves identifying keywords or descriptors to guide your review of the literature. Begin by creating a preliminary working title for your study that focuses on what it is you want to know. Because it's a working title, it can always be revised. Also, state a central research question that describes the variables or concepts you need to examine in your literature review. Forcing yourself to write your topic as a single question requires you to bring it into clearer focus. Then, identify the key concepts in your title and central research question. The following are some examples:

- What effect does parental involvement have on the dropout rate of bilingual middle school students?

- What are the differences between Mexicans and Mexican Americans in their perceptions of and feelings toward their pets?

- How does language use shape the identity of language-minority students?

Precise questions such as these help focus and guide the literature review. Depending on the complexity of your research, you may require several research questions to incorporate all of the variables or concepts you wish to examine in your dissertation. Also include alternative ways of phrasing and expressing concepts and ideas by consulting subject dictionaries and encyclopedias for the common terminology in your study area. Using an index or thesaurus is also advisable in order to establish useful terms. Various academic disciplines have their own thesauri. Some examples are *Thesaurus of ERIC Descriptors*, *Thesaurus of Psychological Index Terms*, and *Sociological Indexing Terms*.

From your research question(s) and working title, compile a list of keywords or descriptors related to your topic.

What effect does parental involvement have on the dropout rate of bilingual middle school students? Keywords include the following:

- *parental involvement*
- *dropout rate*
- *bilingual*
- *middle school students*

Synonyms for *parental involvement* are *parent participation, mother involvement,* and *father involvement.* Synonyms for *bilingual* include *English as a second language* and *English language learners.*

HELPFUL HINT

It is wise to develop a system to track keywords or descriptors and the corresponding volumes and indexes. One effective way is to create a matrix for each abstract or index you consult. Across the top, include the keywords or descriptors you selected for that reference; down the left margin, list the dates of the volumes, starting with the most recent. As you go through each volume, place a check under the descriptors you used next to the date of the volume you used.

Step 2: Create a Search Query

Once you have identified your keywords, you are ready to create a search query to use in the electronic databases. Using the example from Step 1—"What effect does parental involvement have on the dropout rate of bilingual middle school students?"—you would create a search query that looks like this:

> ("parental involvement" OR "mother involvement" OR "father involvement" OR "parent participation") AND (dropout* OR "drop out*") AND (bilingual OR "English language learner*" OR "English as a second language") AND ("middle school student*" or "junior high school student*")

Boolean Operators

Boolean operators define the relationships between words or groups of words. These commands to the database expand or limit your search by combining terms using the words *and, or,* or *not.* For example, to search for "What effect does alcohol have on college students' self-esteem?" type as your words: *alcohol, college students, self-esteem.*

- *AND* narrows the search by obtaining only those items with both Concept 1 and Concept 2 (*"college students" AND "self-esteem"*)

- *OR* broadens the search by obtaining all items with either Concept 1 or Concept 2 (*"self-esteem" OR "self-confidence"*)

- *NOT* obtains items with Concept 1 but eliminates those with Concept 2 (*"alcohol" NOT "illegal drugs"*)

Notice that multiword phrases were placed inside quotation marks. This is necessary to search for those words in that order as a phrase. Remember to put phrases of two or more words in quotation marks.

Truncation

Through this process, you find variations of keywords by adding a truncation symbol to the root. For example, to retrieve all variations on the root "psycholog" (i.e., to find *psychological, psychologist, psychology*), type

Psycholog*

Truncation symbols vary with different databases (e.g., *, ?, $, !*).

Online Help

Instructions for using electronic databases are built into the system. Look for online help buttons or links such as "advanced search" and "search tips." Consult online help to learn how to enter searches, what truncation symbol to use, how to display results, and how to print or download records.

Internet Search Engines

Once you have identified your keywords and developed appropriate search queries, you then select various search engines in which to input your queries. Search engines are tools designed to scan the internet for sites and pages, which are then stored in indexes or databases. You search the contents of databases by typing selected keywords in the text box located on the search engine's home page. The search engine then retrieves documents that match your keywords and displays the results ranked in order of that engine's relevance.

Comparisons of Search Engines

The three major search engines used today are Google (http://www.google.com), Yahoo! Bing (http://www.bing.com), and Ask.com (http://www.ask.com). A search engine for scholarly or academic links is Google Scholar (http://scholar.google.com). You will find many peer-reviewed articles, books, and so on, as well as how often they are cited in other publications.

There are also specialty search engines and virtual libraries in different disciplines. You can find listings for a variety of specialty search engines at Search Engine Guide (http://www.searchengineguide.com/search-engines.html). Also available is a website by TeachThought that displays 100 search engines for academic research (https://www.teachthought.com/learning/100-search-engines-for-academic-research/).

Evaluating Websites

Since anyone can post information on the internet without any oversight, editing, or fact checking, it is important that you evaluate any information that you find on the internet to determine its credibility and authority before using it in your research. Look at the URL to see if it is a personal website, an educational site, a commercial site, or a nonprofit organization site. Look for authorship of the site (Is there an "About Us" link somewhere on the page?) and when the page was last updated. Does the site try to persuade or to sell something, or is it simply providing information? Is there any bias that you can detect? Can you validate the information through another source?

Searching Blogs

There are a variety of blog search engines available; however, we found Google Blog Search (https://blog.google/products/search/) to be one of the fastest and one that returns posts right on topic. The main focus of Google Blog Search is on relevance, but posts can also be sorted by date (click on the top right of the results page). In addition, you can keep track of new postings in your areas of interest via RSS feeds—short summaries sent from your favorite websites.

Step 3: Identify Relevant Literature Sources

The best place to begin your search is with the databases and indexes in your academic area. They help you identify and locate research articles and other sources of information related to your research topic. A detailed description of available secondary sources is beyond the scope of this book. However, as an example, we list some major resources traditionally used by education and social science researchers. To find resources in your specific academic discipline, do a keyword search in your university library's online catalog for your discipline (e.g., *sociology, psychology, anthropology*) followed by the word *handbook, encyclopedia, bibliography, thesaurus, dictionary, abstract, measures,* and so on. Also, consult with librarians at your university library or with faculty in your graduate program for resources they turn to when beginning a new research project.

In planning your search strategy, it is important to determine which academic disciplines are conducting research in your topic area. It is more than likely that your research overlaps with other disciplines. For example, in the third research question in Step 1—"How does language use shape the identity of language-minority students?"—you must decide which academic disciplines might conduct research on this topic. Possibilities include anthropology, psychology, education, communication, and sociology.

The following list contains a variety of literature sources:

SELECTED MULTIDISCIPLINARY DATABASES
Academic Search Premier (EbscoHost)
Communication & Mass Media Complete (EbscoHost)
Google Scholar (http://scholar.google.com)
Research Library (ProQuest)
Social Sciences Citation Index (Web of Science)
OmniFile Full Text Mega (EbscoHost)
SELECTED ANTHROPOLOGY DATABASES
Anthropology Plus (EbscoHost)
AnthroSource (Wiley)
Anthropological Index Online (Royal Anthropological Institute)
Sociological Abstracts (ProQuest)
SELECTED EDUCATION DATABASES
Education Resources Information Center (ERIC, http://eric.ed.gov/)
Education Research Complete (EbscoHost)
Education Full Text (H. W. Wilson)
Education Database (ProQuest)

(Continued)

(Continued)

SELECTED PSYCHOLOGY DATABASES
PsycArticles (American Psychological Association)
PsycInfo (American Psychological Association)
Psychology Database (ProQuest)
Social Sciences Premium Collection (ProQuest)
SELECTED SOCIOLOGY DATABASES
Sociological Abstracts (ProQuest)
SocINDEX with Full Text (EbscoHost)
Social Sciences Full Text (EbscoHost)
Social Sciences Citation Index (Web of Science)
Social Sciences Premium Collection (ProQuest)
BIBLIOGRAPHIES, ENCYCLOPEDIAS, AND DICTIONARIES
Biographical Dictionary of Social and Cultural Anthropology
The Cambridge Dictionary of Sociology
The Corsini Encyclopedia of Psychology and Behavioral Science
Encyclopedia of Education
Encyclopedia of Leadership
Handbooks and Reviews of Research Literature
Bass and Stogdill's Handbook of Leadership
Handbook of Research on the Education of Young Children
Handbook of Research in Emotional and Behavioral Disorders
The Handbook of Research on Teaching
The Handbook of School Psychology
DISSERTATIONS
American Doctoral Dissertations (print)
Dissertation Abstracts International (print)
Index to Tests Used in Educational Dissertations by Emily Fabiano
Dissertations & Theses Database (ProQuest)
Literature Related to Published and Unpublished Measures
Published Measures (Reviews of Instruments)

DISSERTATIONS
Mental Measurement Yearbook
Buros (http://buros.unl.edu/buros/jsp/search.jsp; free searching, but charges to see review—also available in full text from vendors such as EbscoHost)
PRO-ED Test Review

TESTS IN PRINT
Unpublished Measures (Sample Instruments)
Assessments A to Z: A Collection of 50 Questionnaires, Instruments, and Inventories
Handbook of Family Measurement Techniques (Vol. 3)
Handbook of Organizational Measurement
Handbook of Tests and Measurement in Education and the Social Sciences
Measures for Clinical Practice

SCALES FOR THE MEASUREMENT OF ATTITUDES
These are only a few sources of measurement available. Check with your library and the internet under your specific academic discipline.

BOOKS
Ebrary (full-text electronic books available through subscription by your library)
Google Book Search (http://books.google.com/books?um=1&q=&btnG=Search+Books)
Project Gutenberg (https://www.gutenberg.org/)
WorldCat (http://www.worldcat.org; catalog of library holdings worldwide)

GREY LITERATURE
Grey literature is literature not available through published databases or indexes. It can be in print or electronic formats. These are documents published by governmental agencies, academic institutions, corporations, research centers, professional organizations, and so on. • Working papers • Technical reports

(Continued)

(Continued)

GREY LITERATURE

- Government documents
- Conference or symposia proceedings
- White papers
- Business documents
- Newsletters
- Monographs
- Letters and diaries

While these are not scholarly documents, they can provide up-to-date facts and statistics to broaden knowledge about a particular topic. The downside is that they are often difficult to find, and they must be carefully evaluated, as they are not peer reviewed. One way to locate grey literature is to search the agency or institution that produces the literature; another way is to consult a librarian. For a thorough explanation of grey literature and how to find it, refer to *Doing a Literature Search* by Hart (2004, Chapters 7 and 8). You will also find a selection of web-based resources in grey literature at Grey Literature Network Service (http://www.greynet.org).

Existing Literature Review and Systematic Literature Review Articles

These articles, including meta-analysis and meta-synthesis, consist solely of a literature review and are invaluable sources of data. They provide a good overview of research that has been conducted by synthesizing findings from individual studies. Many peer-reviewed systematic reviews are available in journals as well as databases and other electronic sources. The bibliographic references are also very helpful.

Additional Useful Sources

- American Educational Research Association (http://www.aera.net)
- U.S. Department of Education (http://www.ed.gov)
- WestEd (http://www.wested.org)
- Regional Educational Laboratory Program (http://ies.ed.gov/ncee/edlabs)
- Federal Committee on Statistical Methodology (FCSM; https://nces.ed.gov/FCSM/index.asp)
- U.S. Government Publishing Office (http://www.gpo.gov)

Step 4: Search the Literature and Collect Relevant Materials

Begin your search for relevant literature by searching the databases, indexes, books, and other sources listed in Step 3. Examine your results. Are the materials you are finding relevant? Do you see other keywords you could add or subtract from your search? Do particular authors seem to be conducting research on this topic? Do particular journals seem to be publishing research in this area? Use this information to help you focus your search.

When searching the internet for literature, remember that some information may not be dependable, meaning it has not passed the standards of peer reviewers, journal editors, or book publishers. Creswell (2004) elaborated this point by stating, "Material obtained from Web sites not in national, refereed journals needs to be carefully screened to determine the qualifications of the author, the quality of the writing, and the scope and rigor of data collection and analysis" (p. 104). Once you have reviewed the list of references located in your database searches, the next step is to determine which books and articles are most relevant to your study and collect each primary source. Primary source documents contain the original work of researchers and authors. As a serious researcher, you should not rely solely on secondary sources. They do not always provide reliable information. Secondary sources interpret, analyze, or summarize primary sources. They include such published works as newspapers, encyclopedias, handbooks, conference proceedings, and so on. Your review should be based on primary sources whenever possible.

Collecting primary literature consists of browsing, skimming, reading, and photocopying books and documents related to your study. Two types of literature you should collect for your review are the theoretical literature and the research literature. Since most dissertations have a theoretical base, you need to be familiar with those conceptual areas related to your study. In addition, you must be thoroughly familiar with previous research in your subject area.

Collecting literature is an ongoing process, and you need some mechanism for classifying it into those that have a direct bearing on your topic and those that bear generally on your topic. Since it is not feasible to collect all the titles yielded in your search of secondary sources, you must be selective and choose only those most relevant to your study. Always keep in mind your study's purpose. As you gather and sort documents, ask yourself, *How does this relate to my problem?* One strategy is to categorize each book or article as either *very important, moderately important,* or *somewhat important* to your study.

Keeping Track of Pertinent Documents: Organizing Strategies

It is helpful to keep a record of each book or document you consult. With so many to read, you can easily lose track of those already reviewed. You should prepare bibliographic citations for each. One simple way is to list the bibliographic information on index cards and keep them arranged alphabetically by the last name of the author. Another way is to simply maintain an ongoing record of the bibliographic data on your computer. Reference management software programs you download to your computer, such as EndNote, ProCite, Connotea, and Zotero, enable you to create a list of citations, and they automatically convert them into the appropriate style format. The newest release of Microsoft Word also allows you to choose a citation style format, such as American Psychological Association (APA). Reference management databases, such as RefWorks, store your citations on their server and allow you to access your records from any computer that has access to the internet. Check with your library or your graduate program to see which programs they provide or support.

At this point, you must decide on the specific bibliographic style you plan to use in your dissertation. We recommend that you consult with your advisor on this issue. Many universities have preferred styles of citation.

A second organizing strategy is to develop a two-dimensional matrix in which you identify the variables or key descriptors in each publication you consult. To do this, list your variables or descriptors across the top of the page. Then, down the left-hand side of the page, list each reference and its publication date. You can then place a checkmark where the variable and reference intersect.

Not only does this process help you keep track of your reading in the literature, but it also helps you initially select the variables and key concepts you might wish to study. It also is a good mechanism for developing your research instruments.

A variation of this organizing strategy is the author–subtopic matrix in which you note the specific pages on which subtopic information can be located. This is accomplished by putting the page numbers across from the subtopic and under the correct author. After locating pertinent articles for review, you should download the full text to your computer's hard drive or to a portable storage device such as a flash drive or external hard drive. If the articles are in a print journal, photocopy them to read at a more convenient time. We suggest you make a complete photocopy of all articles central to your topic, especially those you want to cite.

Dissertations directly relating to your study can be purchased from ProQuest's Dissertation Copy Options (http://www.proquest.com/products-services/dissertations/order-dissertation.html). Before purchasing, check with your university library; the full text of dissertations may be available to you at no additional charge through the ProQuest Dissertations & Theses database. Other dissertations not available in the library might be obtained through the interlibrary loan process.

Step 5: Critically Read and Analyze the Literature

While collecting your literature, it is necessary to read it critically. This involves questioning, speculating, evaluating, thinking through, and analyzing what you read. What original insights can you gather about your topic that are not stated in any of the references? What important facts and opinions relate to your study? Are there important issues that are not well addressed? You must be able to evaluate and integrate the material you read.

Noting and Summarizing References

1. Do an in-depth reading of your very important publications first so you can understand them thoroughly. Highlight important parts and write down any ideas, insights, or questions that come to you while reading. You can also write on sticky notes or make notations in the margins.

2. For every book or article you read, write a brief summary in your own words that illustrates the essential points. Also include inferences you can make about your study and conclusions you can draw from the book or article.

3. Be sure to accurately record the bibliographic reference exactly as it will appear in the final reference list placed in the dissertation. Include the library call number if your reference is a library book.

4. Develop a coding system so you can identify the type of materials contained on each summary sheet. Usually, this is done by your variables, key topics, or by the descriptors used in locating the references. Write the name of the reference item at the top of the sheet.

5. As you are reading, be alert for quotations that might be useful in presenting your review. If you find quotable material, be sure to copy it carefully with the quotation marks and include the page from which it was taken. Including quotation marks helps you remember which statements are direct quotations. You do not want to inadvertently plagiarize others' ideas. Too often, students overuse quotations in their dissertations. Try to limit the number of direct quotations.

6. Place your summaries in a computer file and then print it out, leaving wide margins. You now have a complete record of what the literature stated about the variables or key concepts in your study.

7. Read through your summaries and look for important themes, big issues, commonalities, and differences. Make notations in the margins of your summary sheets. This provides the basis for developing a logical, coherent outline.

A technique that can be used in preparation for synthesis writing is to build tables to summarize the literature. Building tables is an effective way to overview, organize, and summarize the literature. In their book, *Writing Literature Reviews,* Galvan and Galvan (2017) provide examples on how to build summary tables, such as a table of definitions, key terms, and concepts; a table of research methods; a table of research results; or a table that summarizes theories relevant to your study. Other tables could summarize related quantitative or qualitative studies. Many kinds of tables can be developed to help you get a comprehensive overview of the literature, which is quite useful in the early stages of synthesizing literature.

Step 6: Synthesize the Literature

After you have critically read and analyzed the collected literature, it is time to synthesize the ideas and information you gathered. *Synthesizing* involves comparing, contrasting, and merging disparate pieces of information into one coherent whole that provides a new perspective. This works much like a jigsaw puzzle: The individual pieces of information are placed into a new whole, creating an original work. Critical synthesis is difficult for students to achieve. Too often, students discuss the literature as a chain of isolated summaries of previous studies, such as "White says," "Smith found," and "French concluded" with no attempt to explain the relationship among them or to compare what is being studied. Like individual beads on a necklace, they string together a series of annotations that describe the current state of knowledge about the study but fail to organize the material. This reflects a shotgun approach and misses the point of an integrated literature review. Remember, books and articles are not bricks with mortar banding them together. You need to create the mortar.

A high-quality literature review reflects a careful analysis of all sources and a critical synthesis in which you show how previous studies and information are related to each other and to your study. Describing trees represents the analysis process; describing the forest is the synthesis process and involves "creating a unique new forest" (Galvan, 2006, p. 72). You synthesize the literature when you do the following:

- Identify relationships among studies (such as which ones were landmark studies leading to subsequent studies).

- Compare (show commonalities) and contrast (show differences) the works, ideas, theories, or concepts from various authors.

- Comment on the major themes and patterns you discovered.

- Show evidence of common results using data from multiple sources.

- Discuss the pros and cons of the issues.

- Explain a conflict or contradiction among different sources.

- Point out gaps in the literature, reflecting on why these exist based on the understandings you gained in reading in your study area.

- Note inconsistencies across studies over time.

- Make generalizations across studies.

- Discuss how and why ideas about your topic have changed over time.

- Make connections among the sources cited.

- Discuss literature that has a direct bearing on your area of study.

Before you can write a good synthesis, however, you must first recognize the main points and key ideas of the sources you use. Then, as you read through your written summaries, identify the major themes, trends, or patterns and the big issues, commonalities, and differences among the different authors, and identify your own insights that go beyond what anyone else said. When you do this, you bring your own voice forward rather than that of the authors cited. After all, this is your study and, therefore, it is your responsibility to make sense of the literature to help readers see the information and your topic in a new way and in greater depth. The bottom line is to critique the literature; don't duplicate it.

This sounds easier than it is, for rarely are these trends, patterns, and so on spelled out in the literature. They become apparent to you as you develop insight into the big picture that has emerged over time.

Techniques for Synthesizing the Literature

Various techniques can be used to synthesize the literature. This section provides an overview of some of these techniques. One useful technique we use with doctoral students is a *synthesis matrix*. A synthesis matrix chart identifies themes and patterns or arguments across sources. The top of the matrix lists the various sources of comparison (by author or article), and the side represents the common themes, arguments, or main ideas identified in the articles. See Figure 9.1.

Figure 9.1   Visionary Leadership Synthesis Matrix

COMMON THEMES	SOURCE 1	SOURCE 2	SOURCE 3	SOURCE 4	SOURCE 5
Vision is a key element in both charismatic and transformational leadership theories.	✓		✓		
The visioning process includes at least two stages: creating the vision and communicating the vision.		✓			✓
Visions are best developed collaboratively.	✓		✓	✓	
Definitions of vision include the ideas of providing direction and purpose.	✓		✓		✓
Vision seems vital to an organization's success.		✓			
The outcome of the vision is commitment.			✓		✓
Metaphors used: "Glue" that holds the school together, etc.	✓			✓	

A synthesis matrix such as this helps you begin to link studies together and identify the themes and patterns that appear across your literature sources.

Another useful technique for synthesis writing is to bring your own voice to the foreground. According to Ridley (2012), this means presenting your own voice assertively by

> taking control of the text and leading your reader through the content. This can be done by making your own assertions with appropriate citations to provide support, and by including explicit linking words and phrases to show connections between citations and the different sections and chapters in the text. (pp. 157–158)

Ridley's book, *The Literature Review: A Step-by-Step Guide for Students*, provides rich examples on how to use language and citations to foreground your own voice in writing your literature review.

Constructing a "literature map" is an idea promoted by Creswell (2009) in his book, *Research Design: Qualitative, Quantitative, and Mixed Methods Approaches*. This technique provides a visual summary of the literature—a figure or drawing. Not only does this technique provide an overview of the existing literature, it also "helps you see overlaps in information or major topics in the literature and can help you determine how a proposed study adds to or extends the existing literature rather than duplicates past studies" (p. 107).

You could also create a summary chart of the literature using a concept mapping program. A concept map is a diagram showing the relationships among concepts. Concepts, usually represented as boxes or circles, are connected with labeled arrows in a downward-branching hierarchical structure revealing relationships and patterns among concepts.

Step 7: Organize the Literature

Once the analysis and synthesis of the literature are complete, you must consider how your review will be organized and written. Of primary importance is that your review be structured in a logical and coherent manner. Too often, discussions of related literature are disorganized ramblings. There is no design, no structure that organizes and integrates the material discussed. The following are some guidelines for organizing your review.

Select an Organizational Framework

Prior to writing your first draft, you need to decide on an organizational structure for your review. There are a variety of organizational principles available to structure your literature review. Below are some examples that are commonly used in social science research.

a. *Chronological*—the "acorn to oak" approach. Organizing your review chronologically means that you group and discuss your sources in order of their appearance (usually publication), highlighting the emergence of a topic over a period of time. This approach is useful for historical research or other studies where time is an important element.

b. *Thematic*—the "four schools of thought" or "six themes that emerge" approach. Organizing your review thematically means discussing your sources in terms of themes, topics, important concepts, or major issues. This approach integrates the literature and depends on your ability to synthesize information effectively.

c. *General to Specific*—the "V" or "funnel" approach. First, discuss general material to provide a comprehensive perspective. Last, discuss material most closely related to your study. Rudestam and Newton (2015) used the metaphor of filmmaking to explain this approach. They discussed "long shots and close-ups" to display the degrees of depth required relative to the closeness and relevance of the literature to your study. *Long shots* refer to a topic's background information and are described more generally. *Medium shots* are those sources more closely related to your study and are critiqued in more detail. *Close-ups* refer to those sources with direct bearing on your study, thus requiring a more critical examination.

Create a Topic Outline

If you want your review to be coherent, logical, and well organized, create a topic outline. It helps to do this prior to writing; however, don't be surprised if it changes as you write. In writing your outline, first list the main topics and the order in which they should be presented. Then, under each heading, determine the logical subheadings. Adding additional subheadings depends on the complexity of your problem. The outline helps you see headings that need rearranging to create a logical flow of thought.

With a completed outline, you can sort your references under their appropriate subheadings. Then you must decide in which order the headings should be presented. It is a challenging task to combine and interpret the literature into a well-organized and unified picture of the state of knowledge in your area.

HELPFUL HINT

Create a file for each heading and subheading in your outline. Save the articles and notes related to each heading or subheading in a folder.

Step 8: Write the Literature Review

Pretend your literature review is a discussion with a friend regarding what authors have written about your problem area. Basically, your review is an informative story of what is known about your topic—a summary of the state of the art. You should write for an audience who is intelligent but not knowledgeable about your study. This means limiting (as much as possible) jargon and specialized nomenclature.

Style Manuals

Most universities require consistent use of a particular style manual to format your dissertation document and to cite references. Those widely used in the social sciences include the following:

- American Psychological Association. (2020). *Publication manual of the American Psychological Association* (7th ed.). https://apastyle .apa.org/products/publication-manual-7th-edition
- University of Chicago. (2017). *The Chicago manual of style: The essential guide for writers, editors, and publishers* (17th ed.). https:// www.chicagomanualofstyle.org/home.html

Following are additional helpful resources:

- Oxford English Dictionary, https://www.oed.com
- Purdue University Online Writing Lab (Purdue OWL), https://owl.purdue.edu/owl/purdue_owl.html
- Wordnik, https://www.wordnik.com
- The Brain Mind-Mapping Tool, https://www.thebrain.com
- Docear—The Academic Literature Suite (created by doctoral and postdoctoral students), http://www.docear.org

We highly recommend that you become familiar with your required style manual and begin using it consistently in writing your literature review as well as other sections of your dissertation. It's not as easy as it seems to learn the nuances of headings, in-text citations, end-of-text references, footnotes, and tables and figures. Mastering these techniques early saves you considerable time and effort in the long run.

Techniques for Writing the Literature Review

Typically, a review of the literature begins with a brief introduction that explains the presentation of your literature review—what it is about, the scope, and the organizational structure you selected.

Following the introduction, present the various sections where you review and synthesize the literature.

For each subsection, write an introduction and then describe the information and relevant studies (e.g., "This section is organized chronologically to provide a perspective of trends in the formal evaluation of school superintendents").

Use Headings and Subheadings

This helps the reader follow your train of thought. Usually, headings reflect your study's major variables or themes found in the literature.

Employ Summary Tables

Where considerable research exists, summary tables help cut through a huge mass of literature. Such a table might look like the following:

RESEARCH ON COGNITIVE COACHING CLASSROOMS		
SOURCE	SUBJECTS	RESULTS

You can modify this table format by including other topics of comparison, such as methodology or conclusions.

Use Transitional Phrases

Such phrases guide the reader from one paragraph to the next. It is important that you make strong connections between what has already been reviewed and the material that follows.

Summarize

Pull together each major section with a brief summary at the end. Summaries highlight and clarify the main points of a section, especially if it is long and complex. Conclude by highlighting and summarizing the key points made throughout the literature review.

Emphasize Relatedness

Remember to link studies together by comparing the similarities and differences among them. To keep from boring the reader, be sure to use transitions to integrate paragraphs.

If several studies say essentially the same thing, it is not necessary to describe each one. You can make a summary statement followed by all the related references; for example, "Several studies have found . . . (Brown, 2015; Jones, 2017; Smith, 2018)." Be careful not to ignore studies that contradict other studies. You may evaluate them and try to figure out a plausible explanation (e.g., "Contrary to these studies is the work of Smith and Jones (2016), who found . . .").

Advice on Writing a Literature Review

1. Be Thorough

Include both computer and hand searches; avoid shortcuts. You must cover the full scope of the field. A solid literature review establishes you as an expert and provides a strong background to your research effort.

2. Write with Authority

You are in charge of your literature review, so develop a critical perspective in discussing others' work. Cite relevant authors to emphasize your argument or to provide notable examples of the point you are making. Don't start a paragraph with someone else's name; rather, start each paragraph with the point you wish to make, followed by studies and examples that illustrate and enhance your point.

3. Critique Rather Than Just Report the Literature

You must evaluate and integrate the material you read. Compare and contrast the various studies related to your problem. Comment on the major themes and issues you discovered. In other words, bring meaning to the literature you review; don't just review what has been reported.

4. Avoid Excessive Use of Quotations

Use quotations only when the material quoted is impactful, stated in a unique way, or can be inserted without impairing the continuity of your writing. An accumulation of quotations linked by a sentence or two results in a review that is disjointed and difficult to read.

5. Be Selective

Avoid the temptation to report everything you read. A literature review is not a collection of every book and article relating to a topic. Include only material directly related to your study's purpose and the necessary background to your variables. All the books and articles you read were necessary to help you become an expert in your study area. Like in a courtroom, all the admissible evidence presented must pertain directly to the case and question at hand.

6. Be Careful Not to Plagiarize

Plagiarizing means using someone else's words without quotation marks, closely paraphrasing others' sentences, and stating others' ideas as if they were yours. Remember to always acknowledge another's ideas whenever you cite or borrow them.

7. Critique the Literature; Don't Duplicate It

It is your job to organize and summarize references in a meaningful way. Don't quote long passages or cite others' ideas and words at length. First, present your own review followed by a paraphrase or short, direct quotations. Use long quotations only for a good reason.

8. Use Primary Sources

Primary sources give you information straight from the horse's mouth. They are preferable to secondary sources that are the interpretation of another's work. Find the original books and articles and read them yourself. If you cannot locate the original source, then follow your style manual's guidelines for citing secondary sources. Later in this chapter is a literature review checklist to assess the quality and thoroughness of your literature review.

Helpful Technologies for Searching the Literature and Collaboration

To help in your literature review, consider some technology currently on the market. For example, to personally track your reading, scanners can be very helpful. They scan any papers, ranging from a receipt to multipage documents. Two popular scanner apps for your smartphone are TurboScan and Scanner Pro. They can be downloaded from Google Play for Android users and the App Store for iPhone users. Smartphones can also be used as digital recorders. The Notes app allows you to talk right into your phone and take a note.

The digital tablet is another technology item to consider. You can make handwritten notes directly onto the screen as you would with pen and paper. It is especially useful for drawing graphics that might be difficult to do with a mouse. Your notes and graphics can then be transferred to your computer.

Another helpful tool in writing your dissertation is speech recognition software. This software enables a computer to respond to the human voice in place of a keyboard or mouse. You talk, it types! Wikipedia provides a helpful list of speech recognition software for different platforms (https://en.wikipedia.org/wiki/List_of_speech_recognition_software).

Collaboration

When collaborating with dissertation support groups, individual colleagues, the librarian, or your professors, you might consider the following technologies:

1. **A webcam**: Logitech (http://www.logitech.com/en-us/product/hd-pro-webcam-c920?crid=34) has a very inexpensive yet good quality camera.

2. **Google Drive** is available as part of the G Suite. Document sharing allows for sharing and collaborating. Remember to set the settings to *edit* or *view*, depending on your preference.

3. **Video and web conferencing** platforms provide opportunities for students to collaborate from anywhere. There are several to choose from, and most allow for an audio call, which allows for better communication quality. Some also allow for screen sharing, which allows students to collaborate on documents. Here are a few of the most often utilized: Zoom (https://zoom.us), Skype (https://www.skype.com/en/), and Adobe Connect (http://www.adobe.com/products/adobeconnect.html).

Tips to Keep You Sane and Productive

As you use your computer to write your dissertation, these tips will prove invaluable:

1. Become familiar with your computer software and accessories *before* beginning your dissertation research. Familiarity with technology resources saves you much time and frustration and improves the appearance of your dissertation.

2. Use your required style manual at the outset. It's much easier and saves considerable time if you develop the habit of citing information in the correct style rather than having to revise it later.

3. Computers crash at very inopportune times, so be sure to back up all your files regularly on flash drives, external hard drives, CDs, or DVDs. Be sure to place them in a location safe from fire, flood, theft, or other catastrophes. You might keep one at the office, at a friend's house, or in a safe-deposit box. Your work is too valuable to lose. Remember that Murphy's law also prevails in the research world.

4. Save your work as you go along. After every few sentences, click "Save." You won't regret it. Word processing programs such as Word have a "Save Auto Recover" function. The user can define the frequency down to every one minute. Go to "Word Options" and "Save," then click in the "Save Auto Recover info every: ___ minutes" box and change the time to one minute.

5. Buy a surge protector to plug your computer into in case of electricity blackouts or surges. A better protective device is an uninterruptible power supply (UPS). This device allows your computer to keep running for a short time when power is lost. It contains a battery that kicks in when it senses a loss of power, which gives you time to save any data you are working on. When power surges occur, a UPS intercepts the surge so it doesn't damage your computer.

6. Before making revisions, copy your draft into another file with a different name and date it. This way, you can keep your original drafts intact. You may decide later that an earlier version was best.

7. Do not borrow software. First of all, it is illegal; second, viruses can appear and cause great havoc.

8. Purchase a high-quality antivirus protection program. Antivirus protection software such as Symantec's Norton Antivirus and McAfee are designed to prevent or block viruses, worms, Trojan Horses, and so on.

REMEMBER

"If anything can go wrong, it will!"

"If there is a possibility of several things going wrong, the one that will cause the most damage will be the one to go wrong."

Corollary: "If there is a worst time for something to go wrong, it will happen then."

9. Purchase firewall software if you have a DSL- or cable-connected system. It protects you from hackers. The following are three excellent options:

Symantec	http://www.symantec.com
BlackICE PC Protection	http://www.malavida.com/en/soft/blackice-pc-protection/
ZoneAlarm	http://www.zonealarm.com

These can all be downloaded. Symantec offers free downloads. BlackICE PC Protection can be downloaded for purchase. ZoneAlarm has several options available for download and purchase. Firewalls can create access problems with proxy servers, so beware!

10. Pay attention to your physical self while sitting at the computer. Set your computer up ergonomically and use a proper ergonomic chair and good posture. To learn how to set up your workspace for good ergonomics, refer to Pascarelli's (2004) *Dr. Pascarelli's Complete Guide to Repetitive Strain Injury: What You Need to Know About RSI and Carpal Tunnel Syndrome.*

11. Consider purchasing a glare protector for your screen to help with eyestrain. You can also purchase blue light glasses, which are designed to ease eyestrain when working on a computer or other screen.

12. Take frequent breaks. Stretch, go for a walk, or play with your dog.

Literature Review Checklist

After writing the first draft of the literature review, use the following checklist to assess the thoroughness and quality of what you wrote. Before sending it to your advisor, ask a critical friend to read and comment on your review. Your advisor will be eternally grateful! A well-thought-out, well-written, and interesting review of the literature is a joy to read.

Please note that the items in this checklist comprise a generic set of to-dos when designing a literature review. Not all the items are relevant for all reviews. Select only those that fit your particular situation and use them as a guide.

_____ The literature review is comprehensive (covers the major points of the topic).

_____ There is balanced coverage of all variables in the study.

_____ The review is well organized. It flows logically. It is not fragmented.

_____ The writer critically analyzes the literature instead of stringing together a series of citations.

_____ There is a logical correspondence between the introduction chapter and the literature review.

_____ At least three-fourths of the review focuses on the variables or concepts identified in the purpose statement and research questions. The remaining one-fourth sets the stage and gives the big picture and background to the study.

_____ For each variable or concept, there is some historical and current coverage; the emphasis is on current coverage.

_____ The review relies on empirical research studies, not opinion articles in pop journals.

_____ The review contains opposing points of view (especially if the researcher has a strong bias).

_____ There is a summary at the end of each major section as well as at the end of the chapter.

_____ Primary sources are used in the majority of citations.

_____ There is an appropriate amount of paraphrasing and direct quotation.

_____ The direct quotations do not detract from the readability of the chapter.

_____ Authors who make the same point are combined in the citation.

_____ The review synthesizes and integrates meaning to the literature; it is not a catalog of sources.

SUMMARY

It is important to read and analyze the literature surrounding your study as early as possible in the dissertation process. To do this efficiently, you should thoroughly familiarize yourself with the library and various online search tools. There are eight basic steps for conducting a literature review:

1. Identify keywords or descriptors.

2. Create a search query.

3. Identify relevant literature sources.

4. Search the literature and collect relevant materials.

5. Critically read and analyze the literature.

6. Synthesize the literature.

7. Organize the literature.

8. Write the literature review.

Learning to use the internet and technology efficiently saves considerable time in conducting your literature search. Presenting the results of a literature review is a challenging task. To create a well-organized and integrated review, you should first create a topic

(Continued)

(Continued)

outline to help provide a logical flow of thought. In presenting the review, employ techniques such as headings and subheadings, summary tables, transition phrases, and summaries. It is important that you critique and bring meaning to the literature rather than only reporting what others say.

RESOURCES

Bibme

- https://www.bibme.org/

Creately

- https://creately.com/

Creately, "Conceptual Framework," by Library Admin

- https://creately.com/diagram/example/hm5vuu023/conceptual-framework

Google Sheets

- https://www.google.com/sheets/about/

YouTube, "Google Sheets—Tutorial 01—Creating and Basic Formatting," by Flipped Classroom Tutorials

- https://www.youtube.com/watch?v=QTgvX5MLPC8

Microsoft Word

- https://www.microsoft.com/en-us/microsoft-365/word

Microsoft, APA, MLA, Chicago—Automatically Format Bibliographies

- https://support.microsoft.com/en-us/office/apa-mla-chicago-automatically-format-bibliographies-405c207c-7070-42fa-91e7-eaf064b14dbb?ui=en-us&rs=en-us&ad=us

TeachThought: The Top 100 Search Engines for Academic Research

- https://www.teachthought.com/learning/search-engines/

Zoom

- https://www.zoom.us/

Writing the Research Methods 10

As for the search for truth, I know from my own painful searching, with its many blind alleys, how hard it is to take a reliable step, be it ever so small, towards the understanding of that which is truly significant.

—Albert Einstein

The Research Methodology

Beginning the climb on the dissertation mountain involves choosing a dissertation topic, conducting a review of the literature, and selecting and describing a research methodology. These are not linear processes; they undulate back and forth and often go on simultaneously. Reviewing the literature grounds you in understanding what is known and not known about your study's topic and helps provide the basis for selecting an appropriate method. Whatever methodology you choose, you need to understand the techniques and processes specific to that method.

Research methodology can be classified under three broad generic categories: *quantitative, qualitative,* or *multiple methods* (also called *mixed methods*). Multiple/mixed methods contains quantitative and qualitative methods; however, either quantitative or qualitative methods is generally more prominent. Within the broad categories of quantitative, qualitative, or multiple methods, a variety of designs exist with their own protocol for collecting and analyzing data. The information presented here focuses on quantitative and qualitative methods, since multiple/mixed methods includes both.

Considerations for Methods Selection

Students frequently ask, "How do I go about selecting the method for my study?" The answer isn't simple; it is possible to identify several different methodological approaches for a single topic. Methodology selection rests primarily on the (1) problem and research question to be investigated, (2) purpose of the study, (3) theory base (including prior research), and (4) nature of the data. We recommend that at least one of your dissertation committee members possesses the expertise in the methodology you select. How comfortable are you with statistics? Do you have the required complex abstract thinking skills necessary for qualitative research? It is essential for a quality dissertation that you are able to write clearly and precisely. As you begin this process, it's common to feel a bit uncomfortable with your level of knowledge about research methodology or with the skills required to conduct a research study. In our experience, few students remember well all of the content from their research methodology courses or come to the dissertation process confident about their ability to apply research skills. Students often find that learning by doing plays a large role in the process. With guidance from your committee, your learning evolves over time as you proceed through each stage of the dissertation. It is important that the design provides a vehicle for informing the research. In other words, don't try to make your study fit a predetermined research methodology.

The research approach you select for your study will be quantitative, qualitative, or a combination of the two, referred to as *multiple* or *mixed methods*. In this section, we present considerations related to the qualitative and quantitative paradigms. This book, however, is not a methodology text, and we suggest that, along with discussing the appropriate method for your study with your dissertation advisor, you revisit the books and articles from your research courses. You can also refer to the resource section at the end of this chapter for additional sources related to methodology.

Differences between Quantitative and Qualitative Research

What is the difference between qualitative and quantitative research? Staindack and Staindack (1988) explained it this way: "Qualitative research differs from quantitative research in its theoretical/philosophical rationale" (p. 4). In philosophical terms, the quantitative approach is referred to as *logical positivism*.

In quantitative research, inquiry begins with a specific plan—a set of detailed questions or hypotheses. Researchers seek facts and causes of behavior and want to know about the variables so differences can be identified. They collect data that are primarily numerical using mathematical, statistical, and computational procedures through surveys, tests, experiments, and so on. Quantitative approaches manipulate variables and control the research setting. Common quantitative designs include experimental research, quasi-experimental research, nonexperimental research, ex-post facto/causal comparative research, and correlational research.

The qualitative approach focuses on people's experience from their perspective and is based on the following philosophical constructs: *ontology*—the nature of reality, *epistemology*—how the researcher knows what they know, *axiology*—values, *rhetoric*—the research language, and *methodology*—the research procedures (Creswell, 2007; Denzin & Lincoln, 2011). Inquiry begins with questions about the area under investigation. Researchers seek an inclusive picture—a comprehensive and complete understanding of the topic they are studying. They may make observations; conduct in-depth, open-ended, or semi-structured interviews; or review written documents, photographs, videos, performances, or cultural objects such as art. Rather than numbers, the data are mainly words and can also be audible or visual objects that describe people's knowledge, opinions, perceptions, and feelings as well as detailed descriptions of people's actions, behaviors, activities, and interpersonal interactions. Qualitative research may also focus on organizational processes.

> Nothing in life is to be feared, it is only to be understood.
>
> —Marie Curie

Researchers can go into a setting or use technology to collect data. Qualitative researchers look at the essential character or nature of something, not necessarily the quantity. This approach is sometimes called *naturalistic inquiry* because the research involves real-world issues and settings. Researchers are interested in the meanings people attach to the activities and events in their world and are open to whatever emerges. Similar to quantitative research, *qualitative research* is the general term that includes several research designs, such as case study research, historical research, ethnography, grounded theory, and narrative research.

The most salient differences between qualitative and quantitative approaches are listed in Table 10.1.

Table 10.1 Comparing Research Methods	
QUALITATIVE	**QUANTITATIVE**
• Naturalistic designs	• Experimental designs
• Observations/interviews/ images	• Explanatory
• Inductive (can also be deductive) analysis	• Deductive analysis (test hypotheses)
• The researcher is the instrument	• Standardized measures
• Credibility	• Validity depends on careful instrument construction
• Depth and breadth of data	• Reliability
• Dependability	• Large samples (random sampling)
• Small samples	• Breadth (limited set of variables measured)
• Discovering/exploring/ examining/substantiating concepts	• Testing/verifying/quantifying
• Extrapolations	• Generalizations
• Making meaning	

Both research orientations play an important role in extending knowledge. Whichever you select for your study, be sure to read widely in that methodological area so you are knowledgeable about the data collection and analysis procedures necessary to conduct your study. Remember, in the end, you must justify your choice of method and clarify why it was the best way to conduct your study. Because there are no inferential statistics to be performed in qualitative research, some students mistakenly believe it to be easier to conduct than a quantitative study. This is not true! Analyzing large amounts of qualitative data into meaningful themes and patterns can be a sizable task requiring considerable time and effort.

Multiple Methods

Although qualitative and quantitative approaches are grounded in different paradigms, it is possible to combine them in the same study. The multiple methods approach is a viable method in the social and human sciences, evidenced by a variety of books and journals reporting and promoting this type of research. In the past two decades, there has been an increase in the number of articles and texts about procedures for conducting multiple methods studies (Creswell, 2009; Tashakkori & Teddlie, 2003).

If appropriate for the research, you can incorporate both qualitative and quantitative approaches into a single study. Generally, researchers select quantitative methodology or qualitative methodology as the primary method in multiple methods study design. For example, in a study that is mainly quantitative, you can gather numerical data from a large sample using a survey instrument to get a broad perspective and then select a few participants to study by observing and recording their behaviors. If you select a qualitative method as the primary design, you can gather data through participant interviews and then collect numerical data, such as a Likert scale questionnaire, to add another dimension to the results.

As in any design choice, it's important to present a rationale for combining methods. Qualitative and quantitative approaches in a single study can complement each other by providing results with greater breadth and depth. Combining *what* with a possible *why* can add support for your findings. With quantitative methods, you can summarize large amounts of data and reach generalizations based on statistical projections. In contrast, qualitative research recounts the lived experience of a smaller sample in an effort to provide rich, descriptive detail.

Gay and Airasian (2003) offer a practical resource for understanding how to combine qualitative and quantitative methods:

1. The QUAL–Quan model, where qualitative data are collected first and are more heavily weighted than quantitative data.

2. The QUAN–Qual model, where quantitative data are collected first and are more heavily weighted than qualitative data.

3. The QUAN–QUAL model, where qualitative and quantitative data are equally weighted and are collected concurrently. (pp. 184–185)

Whichever design you select for your study, research studies generally proceed with the introduction, problem, questions, literature support, methods (including data collection and analysis), and interpretation and reporting of results, implications, and conclusions.

Describing the Methodology

The methodology chapter of a dissertation describes the design and the specific procedures used in conducting your study. It is vital that this section is clear, comprehensive, and sufficiently detailed so that other researchers can adequately judge the results you obtain and can validly replicate the study. In a quantitative study, the methodology chapter usually contains the following sections: introduction, purpose and research questions and/or hypotheses and null hypotheses, research design and reasons for selecting it, protection of human subjects, population and sample, sampling procedures, instrumentation, validity and reliability, data collection procedures, data analysis, data display (e.g., charts, tables, graphs, etc.), and limitations.

Qualitative studies typically use different terminology in describing the methodology section. For example, in a qualitative study, the methodology sections often include the following: the introduction and context of the study, purpose and research questions, rationale for the qualitative design, type of design, ethical considerations (such as protection of human subjects), researcher's role and related issues, site selection, data sources (e.g., population and sample), sampling procedures, data collection techniques, procedures for managing and recording data, data analysis procedures, types of data display (e.g., text, graphics, etc.), strategies to establish credibility, dependability, and limitations. Following is a description of the common sections of a study.

Introduction

You may introduce the methodology chapter several ways, depending on the style preference of your advisor and committee. Generally, there is an opening paragraph introducing the study and stating the chapter's organization. In qualitative studies, this is followed by a brief description of the problem, a restatement of your study's purpose, and research questions. Quantitative research also includes the purpose and research questions and/or null hypotheses and hypotheses. A brief description of the problem would also be included.

Research Design

In this section, state the type of research and design used for the study as well as the rationale for your selection. The research design you select is based on the purpose, research question(s), and nature of your study.

There are several types of qualitative or quantitative method designs to choose from, depending on the goal of your study. Some possible quantitative designs are correlational, ex-post facto, case study, true experimental, and quasi-experimental. Qualitative designs include but are not limited to ethnography, grounded theory, historical, and narrative. Some designs lend themselves to multiple methods, such as case studies or Delphi studies.

Research Ethics and Human Subjects Protection

Human Subjects Protection

In 1974, Congress enacted the National Research Act in response to a number of events that indicated human subjects were being harmed or exploited. The National Research Act of 1974 created the National Commission for Protection of Human Subjects, who subsequently developed a system requiring institutional review board (IRB) approval for human subjects research. The IRB procedures increase autonomy and respect and safeguard those who are vulnerable (Amdur & Bankert, 2002; Creswell & Poth, 2018; Patton, 2015). These policies became known as the *Code of Federal Regulations* (U.S. Department of Health and Human Services, 2010). In 1978, the Commission produced *The Belmont Report*, outlining three main ethical principles and the corresponding IRB requirements for conducting research that involve human subjects, as noted in Table 10.2.

Table 10.2   Main Ethical Principles for Conducting Research With Human Subjects

MAIN PRINCIPLES	CORRESPONDING IRB REQUIREMENTS
1. Respect for Persons	1a. Voluntary consent to participate 1b. Informed consent 1c. Privacy and confidentiality 1d. The right to withdraw from participating without penalty
2. Beneficence	2a. Risks justified by potential benefits 2b. Study design minimizes risks 2c. Conflicts managed to reduce bias
3. Justice	3a. The study doesn't exploit vulnerable persons 3b. The study doesn't exclude people who may benefit from participation 3c. Participation is borne equally by society

Source: Office for Human Research Protections (1979).

Universities and other research institutions such as think tanks have established an IRB charged with reviewing and approving human subjects research according to standards that align with the Code of Federal Regulations. It is important to factor in time for this process because you cannot move forward to collect data until the IRB has approved you to do so. Generally, following a successful proposal meeting and with approval of the dissertation advisor, the researcher is expected to complete an application with information specific to the research study and submit it to the IRB, along with all required forms, including a copy of the certificate indicating the researcher has successfully completed training to protect human subjects. Check with your institution about these requirements, as each university has established policies and procedures for completing this process.

Ethics and the Researcher

Guidelines for ethical practices in conducting research are available from professional academic associations such as the American Psychological Association (APA), the American Educational Research Association (AERA), and so on. In addition to respect for participants, respect should be shown for the research site(s), including gaining permission to collect data at the site, if appropriate.

Researchers are expected to include a discussion regarding any conflicts of interest or biases they may have. As researchers, we bring a certain level of education and experiences that help prepare us to conduct a study; however, those same experiences can alter our perspectives when collecting and/or analyzing data. Therefore, it's important to recognize and acknowledge these areas and to include strategies for mitigating any biases. Doing so demonstrates transparency and builds trust with those who will read your study.

Population and Sample

The population and sample (or data sources) section includes a description of the individuals who participated in your study and the procedures used to select them. There are differences between quantitative and qualitative standards regarding sample size. Ideally, in a quantitative study, an entire population would be used to gather information. However, this is usually not feasible, as most groups of interest are either too large or are less accessible for varied reasons. In qualitative research, the sample size is often smaller, due to the depth and breadth of data collected. When you don't have an opportunity to study a total group, select a sample as representative as possible of the total group in which you are interested.

Gay and Airasian (1996) provided a clear definition of the terms *sampling* and *population* to help to distinguish between the two:

> Sampling is the process of selecting a number of individuals for a study in such a way that the individuals represent the larger group from which they were selected. The individuals selected comprise a sample and the larger group is referred to as a population. (pp. 111–112)

NOTE ABOUT QUALITATIVE RESEARCH SAMPLING

1. Qualitative research participant sample size is smaller than quantitative studies, often limited to single- or double-digit numbers of participants. Literature is available that addresses sample size considerations, depending on the specific method (e.g., ethnography verses grounded theory).

2. In qualitative research, there is less concern for large sample size and more emphasis placed on details of the setting and/or situation, the participants, and rich descriptions of the participant's experiences.

3. Rather than generalizing information, the intent of qualitative research is to discover and illuminate the lived experience associated with the study topic.

NOTE ABOUT QUANTITATIVE RESEARCH SAMPLING

1. The bigger your sample, the more it represents the total population and sample and supports your findings.

2. Before deciding how many to select for your sample, you must know the size of your population so that you can reliably draw the appropriate sample size.

3. Your sample size represents the number of individuals to be contacted for their participation in your study. It does not represent the number of individuals who must respond. However, in quantitative studies, there is literature that supports a certain percentage range for an acceptable sample size response, depending on the field of study, type of research, and population to be studied.

Sampling Procedures

The credibility of your study relies on the quality of the procedures you used to select the sample. These procedures should be described in detail as this contributes to the strength of your findings. Some examples of quantitative sampling are probability sampling, random, or systematic studies. Qualitative sampling examples include purposeful, criterion based, maximum variation, or expert studies. Your description should include the following:

1. The number of individuals included and where they are located

2. Why you selected this particular number

3. The criteria you used for inclusion in the sample

4. A step-by-step account of exactly how you went about selecting your sample

Instrumentation

This section includes a description of instruments used to collect data—surveys, questionnaires, interview questions, observation forms, and so on. Each instrument used should be described in detail in the methodology chapter. The following is a description of relevant information needed for quantitative and qualitative studies.

For quantitative studies, provide the following information (as relevant):

1. Appropriateness of the instrument for your population and setting

2. The validity and reliability of the instruments (*Validity* is the degree to which your instrument truly measures what it purports to measure. In other words, can you trust that findings from your instrument are true? *Reliability* is the degree to which your instrument consistently measures something.)

3. How the instrument is administered and scored

4. Type(s) of statistical methods to be applied and software used (e.g., SPSS)

5. Interrater reliability—measuring the consistency between raters or between a rater and an expert

6. Type(s) of response categories—rating scales, check lists, ranking, and so on

For qualitative studies, provide the following information (as relevant):

1. The alignment of the instrument relative to participants, setting, interviews, documents, artifacts, and/or observations that will inform the research questions

2. The appropriate type of questions that are best suited for your study (e.g., open-ended questions or semi-structured questions). You can also develop follow-up questions, if needed, to increase the depth and breadth of the responses.

3. The credibility and dependability of the instrument (*Credibility* is the degree to which your instrument truly measures what it purports to measure. This can be accomplished by engaging an expert panel to review and comment on the interview questions and/or by conducting a pilot test of a few people that meet the same criteria as the anticipated participants. Dependability demonstrates support for the conclusions.)

4. Strategies you will use to collect the interview responses and/or observation or other data (e.g., note taking, recording, online [written or audio], video, photographs, performance, behaviors, individually, focus group, artifacts, documents, etc.). Develop an interview protocol.

5. How data will be analyzed for themes

6. Dependability process, such as using a second reviewer who independently reviews the responses for consistency using the same coding process as the researcher

NOTE

Whether the method is qualitative, quantitative, or multiple methods, all sample forms of instruments, protocol, assessment forms, and so on should be included as appendixes. Copyrighted instruments cannot be reproduced in a dissertation without written permission. If you wish to use copyrighted instruments, permission should be obtained in writing from the holder of the copyright.

Developing Your Own Instrument

You can use an established instrument (see the resources section at the end of this chapter) or you can develop your own instrument. If you are unable to locate a satisfactory instrument that adequately measures your study's variables or concepts, you may either modify an existing validated instrument or create your own instrument. It is appropriate to change the wording or eliminate questions when modifying an instrument for a different population. However, keep in mind that the changes you make may affect the reliability and validity of the instrument. If you modify an instrument, it is your responsibility to justify the changes made and to provide information about the reliability and validity of the revised instrument. Written permission must be obtained from the copyright holder.

Should you choose to develop a new instrument, recount how it was developed and include a detailed description of the pilot tests that you conducted and the subsequent revisions. Place a copy in the appendix of all the instruments used.

NOTE

When developing items for your instrument, it is critical that you align the items with your research questions to ensure that all research concepts or variables are adequately covered in your instrument. A good technique is to create a matrix in which you display your research questions on the left side and the survey (or other instrument) questions/items on the right (see Table 10.3).

Table 10.3   Matrix Questionnaire Form

RESEARCH QUESTION	CORRESPONDING ITEM/ QUESTION
Research Question 1	Part I: Survey Questions 1–5
	Question 1:
	Question 2:
	Question 3:
	Question 4:
	Question 5:

RESEARCH QUESTION	CORRESPONDING ITEM/ QUESTION
Research Question 2	Part II: Survey Questions 6–10
	Question 6:
	Question 7:
	Question 8:
	Question 9:
	Question 10:
Research Question 3	Part III: Survey Questions 11–15
	Question 11:
	Question 12:
	Question 13:
	Question 14:
	Question 15:

When describing your instrument(s), it is important to explain your rationale for selection. The following is a dissertation example.

EXAMPLE

In an exhaustive review of the literature, the research supporting the use of the SACQ [Student Adaptation to College Questionnaire] far outweighed the criticism of the assessment tool. The SACQ has been used as an assessment tool in more than one hundred dissertations and theses. Even with its limitations, the majority of the research supported the use of the SACQ in understanding student adjustment to college. (Schultz, 2008, p. 110)

Instrument Test

Testing the instrument is important to establish whether the instrument will provide the data that will inform your research questions. This process is referred to variously as a *pilot test, beta test,* or *field test.* For the purposes of this discussion, we will refer to it as a *pilot test.* Whether you create your own instrument or modify an existing one, it should be tested prior to distributing it to your study participants.

One way to accomplish this is to select a small group of people who aren't involved in your study but who match the criteria of the participants in your study. The people that are testing your instrument provide valuable information regarding the validity or the instrument as well as illuminating any design issues, such as the following:

- Understandable instructions

- Clear wording

- Adequate answers

- Sufficient information

- Length

- Convenience

Following the pilot test, it may be necessary to revise your instrument to reflect the various recommendations provided by the test respondents. Be sure to include pilot testing in the instrument section of your methods chapter. Describe the testing process and indicate any revisions that were made to your instrument as a result of the pilot test.

Data Collection Procedures

This section describes the steps you will take to conduct your study and the order in which they occurred. It is important that your writing is clear and precise so that readers understand and other researchers can replicate your study. Your description should state how and when the data were collected.

NOTE

To help you efficiently deal with organizing the data collection, create a data source chart. This chart assists you in tracking the data process (e.g., who received the instrument, when they received the instrument, who completed the instrument, and what/how/when data analysis was performed). Data sources can also be arranged by research questions or hypotheses.

Best Time to Collect Data

When to collect data is a critical issue because it can greatly affect your response rate. It is important for you to consider the availability of your population. For example, there are several windows of opportunity when people are more likely to be available. In many fields, such as education, government, health care, nonprofit, and for profit, potential participants are generally less available near and during holidays.

Data collection always takes longer than you realize. It takes time for participants to respond to surveys, schedule interviews, and engage in follow-up when necessary. Plan ahead to arrange for the best opportunity to successfully collect data.

Data Analysis

This section includes an explanation of how you analyzed the data as well as your rationale for selecting a particular analysis method. If your study is quantitative, for example, report the statistical tests and procedures you used, how they were treated, and the level of statistical significance that guided your analysis. Since statistical tests may vary by research question, you should explain your tests and procedures for each question. An example follows:

> Research questions four through nine focused on the differences in students' attitudes in looped and conventional classrooms. Composite means and standard deviations were computed for each of the attributes: self-concept, motivation, instructional mastery, and sense of control. The data were analyzed using t-test computations to determine if a significant difference existed between students in looped and conventional classrooms on each of the attitudes assessed. (Johnston, 2000, p. 72)

If your study is qualitative, display the data and identify the coding processes used to convert the raw data into themes or categories for analysis. Your description should include specific details about how you managed the large amount of data associated with qualitative analysis. Include information about the use of software, notes, or other processes. This helps readers understand how you reduced and analyzed the data.

There are a variety of approaches that researchers can choose from to code data. There is no one right way to code qualitative data. One example to help you understand the coding process is provided by Creswell (2004). He described five steps for analyzing qualitative text as data:

1. Initially read though the text data.

2. Divide the text into segments of information.

3. Label the segments of information with codes.

4. Reduce the overlap and redundancy of codes.

5. Collapse codes into themes. (p. 238)

A variety of qualitative software products are available for analyzing qualitative data; however, it does take time to learn how to use them well. A book titled *Using Software in Qualitative Research: A Step-by-Step Guide* by Silver and Lewins (2014) is a useful source for information about various software programs.

Validating the Findings

In this section on data analysis, it is important to include how you addressed the issue of validity. Qualitative researchers often use the term *credibility* to refer to the concept of validity and *dependability* to refer to reliability (Lincoln & Guba, 1986; Patton, 2015). Validity in quantitative research or credibility in qualitative research indicates that a research process was used to establish the accuracy of your instrument(s). It's the dependability factor that helps the reader trust your data analysis. There are multiple tactics for establishing reliability related to quantitative research (e.g., interrater reliability) and qualitative research (e.g., using a second reviewer). It's important that you select one that is appropriate to your study and describe it clearly.

Qualitative Research Consistency Review Process

It is important to employ an analysis process to support and strengthen methodological integrity in research. While quantitative researchers use terms such as *validity*, qualitative researchers use terms such as *consistency*. One method of demonstrating consistency includes additional reviewer(s) who are familiar with qualitative research theories and practices and who have experience in graduate research. The additional reviewer(s) is selected for participation in the qualitative coding and analysis process. A 7-step qualitative research consistency review process (Hyatt, 2023) is applied to increase the integrity and consistency of qualitative data analysis:

1. The primary researcher analyzes the data and then meets with the reviewer(s) to explain the coding process for identifying themes. The researcher maintains the highlighted/analyzed version of the transcript.

2. The primary researcher selects a transcript for the purpose of acquainting the reviewer(s) with the coding process. The

reviewer(s) is provided with an unmarked copy of the selected transcript.

3. Prior to analysis, the researcher and reviewer(s) will each read the transcript to (a) familiarize the reviewer(s) with the data from the transcripts, (b) to further the reviewer(s) consideration of the information and, (c) to answer any questions about the transcript.

4. The researcher assists the reviewer(s) in completing the analysis of one selected transcript by bracketing for horizontalization, reduction, and synthesis of the text. Meaning units are entered in the left margin. Structural descriptions and findings are entered into the right margin. This completes analysis of the single transcript.

5. The additional reviewer(s) applies the same process to the remaining transcripts independent of the primary researcher. If there are multiple additional reviewers, each works independently.

6. After completion of the process for all transcripts, the primary researcher and reviewer(s) reconvene. The primary researcher and the reviewer(s) review their identified findings, discuss similarities and differences, and come to a consensus regarding the conclusions. A categorizing form may be created to identify the agreed-upon themes.

7. Generally, criteria for major themes are met when a majority of the participants provided supporting data for the theme(s).

Limitations

Limitations are particular features of your study that you know may affect the results or your ability to generalize the findings. Limitations can involve areas over which you have little or no control. Some typical limitations include population, sample size, regional and cultural differences, constraints associated with methods design, and response rate.

All studies have some limitations, and it is important that you state them openly and honestly so that those reading your dissertation understand them and, most importantly, know that you are aware of them and are being transparent in your willingness to address them.

Methodology Chapter Elements—A Checklist

As you write your first draft of the methodology chapter, consider the following elements. You may find it useful to develop a checklist (such as the example in Table 10.4) and to note each of the elements and the date of completion.

Table 10.4   Example Methods Chapter Checklist

SECTION	NOTES	DATE COMPLETED	✓
INTRODUCTION			
Topic and Context			
Chapter Organization			
PURPOSE AND RESEARCH QUESTION AND HYPOTHESES AND/OR NULL HYPOTHESES			
Purpose Statement			
Research Question and/or Hypotheses/Null Hypotheses			
RESEARCH DESIGN			
Design Type (e.g., qualitative/quantitative/mixed methods)			
Specific Method (e.g., experimental, ethnography, etc.)			
Rationale for Choice			
RESEARCH ETHICS AND HUMAN SUBJECTS PROTECTION			
Importance of Protecting Human Subjects			
*Researcher Training and Certification			
Steps to Protect Human Subjects and Increase Equity			
*Approval by IRB			
*Consent Process (letter, forms, etc.)			
Discuss Researcher Bias			
Describe Strategies to Mitigate Researcher Bias			

POPULATION AND SAMPLE			
Description of Population and Sample			
Sampling Strategies			
Inclusion Criteria			
Number of Participants			
*Procedures to Identify and Recruit Participants			
INSTRUMENTATION			
Detailed Description of Instruments and Protocol			
*Copy of Instruments and Protocol			
Alignment with Study			
*Written Permission of Instrument Author			
Strategies for Quantitative Validity and Reliability and/or Strategies for Qualitative Credibility and Dependability			
Pilot Test/Expert Panel Process Description			
Indicate Revisions Due to Pilot Test or Expert Panel			
DATA COLLECTION			
Describe All Procedures Used to Collect Data			
DATA ANALYSIS			
Explain Statistical Tests or Qualitative Analysis			
Describe the Software Used			
Note How Data Analysis Will Be Reported and Displayed			
LIMITATIONS			
List Limitations			
Describe Impact of Limitations on the Study			

*Check with your university and dissertation advisor for any documents required to be included in the appendix.

SUMMARY

Selecting a methodology requires understanding the two major research paradigms: qualitative and quantitative approaches. Which one you select depends primarily on the problem investigated, the purpose of your study, and the nature of the data. Qualitative studies generate words that describe people's actions, behaviors, and interactions whereas quantitative studies generate numerical data derived from surveys, tests, and experiments. Both approaches can be combined in a single study as multiple/mixed methods.

By describing your methodology clearly and precisely, you will increase confidence in your findings as well as make it possible for other researchers to understand and replicate your study. You must include detailed descriptions about your research design, protection of human subjects, population and sample, sampling procedures, instrumentation, data collection procedures, data analysis, and limitations.

Now that you have completed your introductory and methodology chapters, it is time to meet with your advisor and committee to discuss and critically analyze your proposed study. The next chapter provides some guidelines for holding the proposal meeting.

RESOURCES

Academy of Management, Ethics

- https://aom.org/about-aom/governance/ethics

American Anthropological Association, Code of Ethics

- https://www.americananthro.org/ethics-and-methods

AERA, Professional Ethics

- https://www.aera.net/About-AERA/AERA-Rules-Policies/Professional-Ethics

APA, Ethical Principles of Psychologists and Code of Conduct

- https://www.apa.org/ethics/code/index

APA, Publication Manual of the American Psychological Association

- https://apastyle.apa.org/products/publication-manual-7th-edition

American Sociological Association, Ethics
- https://www.asanet.org/about/ethics

U.S. Copyright Office
- https://www.copyright.gov/

Buros, Mental Measurements Yearbook
- https://buros.org/mental-measurements-yearbook

Office for Human Research Protections, 45 CFR 46
- https://www.hhs.gov/ohrp/regulations-and-policy/regulations/45-cfr-46/index.html

The Office of Research Integrity
- https://ori.hhs.gov/

Qualtrics, Experience Management
- https://www.qualtrics.com/experience-management/research/determine-sample-size/

Sage Research Methods, *Using Software in Qualitative Research: A Step-by-Step Guide* by Christina Silver & Ann Lewins
- https://methods.sagepub.com/book/using-software-in-qualitative-research-2e

The Proposal Meeting 11

The proposal meeting, sometimes referred to as *preliminary proposal* or *prelims*, represents a major step in the dissertation process. This meeting has traditionally been viewed as noteworthy because your committee's approval of your proposal permits you to move forward and collect your data. This represents your transition from doctoral student to doctoral candidate, and many universities refer to this process as *advancement to candidacy*.

At the proposal meeting, you and the committee discuss and critically analyze your proposed study. Important understandings that will determine the ultimate direction of your research and the efficiency with which your study can be completed are reached at this meeting. Your goal is to obtain your committee's approval to move ahead with your study in accordance with the agreements made in the meeting. Universities have dissertation guidelines and established forms that require committee signatures. The proposal meeting likely has a corresponding form that is signed by your committee and includes the results of the proposal meeting along with a summary of revisions necessary for you to move forward.

Acceptable proposals vary according to the preferences of the university, the department, the program, the field of study, and your dissertation advisor. Generally, proposals consist of the front matter (e.g., title page, table of contents, etc.), introductory chapter, literature review chapter, methodology chapter with the proposed research instruments to be used in the study, references, and any appendixes required by your committee and the institution.

NOTE

Be sure to have the writing style manual (e.g., American Psychological Association [APA], or Modern Language Association [MLA]) required by your university as you write your dissertation. Be aware of your institution's policies and writing requirements, such as structure and formatting, writing in future tense or past tense, and writing in first or third person.

Preparing for the Proposal Meeting

One important key to success is self-confidence. An important key to self-confidence is preparation.

—Arthur Ashe

To ensure that committee members have adequate time to review your proposal before the meeting, it is preferable that they receive a final draft according to your university and advisor's preferences. Generally, it's best if you provide the complete written proposal at least two to four weeks prior to the meeting. This draft should incorporate all of their previous recommendations for change. It should also be a well-written, high-quality document—clean, accurate, and complete.

Consult your advisor about preparing for the proposal meeting. Some preparation considerations include the following:

1. Required procedures—consult your university's guidelines and those specific to your department and program

2. Procedures preferred by your advisor

3. Scheduling the meeting, which includes finding a date and time acceptable to all committee members, selecting an appropriate and convenient location for the meeting, and reserving a meeting room

4. Your advisor's expectations for presentation of the proposal information

5. Structure and order of proposal meeting tasks

6. Length of time of the proposal meeting

7. Appropriate dress and decorum for the proposal meeting

NOTE

Your university/program dissertation guidelines are a good source of information. Also, your department and program may have additional required criteria. For example, many institutions require two weeks to a month of lead time in order to schedule the dissertation proposal meeting. It's important to factor this into your planning timeline.

Plan to arrive early to the proposal meeting room to allow for presentation preparation and to familiarize yourself with your surroundings. We also advise that you be well steeped in the literature related to your topic and the methodology you've selected. Not only does it give you greater self-assurance, but it also indicates to your committee that you understand and have control over your study's parameters. Also, consult colleagues experienced in the process and get their perspective about the meeting's dynamics and expectations.

During the Proposal Meeting

Your advisor typically introduces the committee members and facilitates the proposal meeting. Proposal meetings are considered working meetings and are intended to be a discussion between you and your committee, characterized by a spirit of collegiality and support in an effort to strengthen your study. Questions and comments about the proposal revolve around understanding the study, clarifying ambiguities, anticipating problems, and uncovering any major flaws in the study's design and methods. The committee's role is to bring their knowledge of the topic and research experience to assist you in defining the study parameters more clearly and precisely. Before your committee accepts your proposal and sends you off to gather data, committee members will likely address the following:

1. *Scope of inquiry.* Is it manageable? Is it dissertation-level research?

2. *Appropriateness of the design.* Is it suitable for the research questions asked? Is it doable?

3. *Significance of the study.* Does it make a contribution to the field?

4. *Instrumentation.* Will your instrument(s) adequately provide data to inform the research questions?

NOTE

Even though you may have previously received input on your proposal from committee members and revised accordingly, expect changes. The interaction of the committee invokes a synergy that often leads to new ideas and perspectives. Rely on the collective wisdom of your committee to guide you in this initial phase of your research.

The proposal meeting is a good time to discuss and agree on the expectations and procedures to which you will adhere during the remainder of the study. By agreeing on the following, your work together should be smoother, more efficient, and less ambiguous.

1. What are the required proposal revisions?

2. Who should review the revisions (e.g., only the advisor, other committee members)?

3. What is the timeline for sending the revisions to the appropriate committee members for review?

4. When should you expect to hear back about the review of the revisions?

5. If the revisions are minor and don't impact the methodology section, can you continue to move forward and apply to the institutional review board for approval to collect data?

At the conclusion of the proposal meeting, the advisor summarizes the committee's decisions and recommendations for changes. This ensures understanding about what was said and agreed on.

After the Proposal Meeting

Immediately following the proposal meeting, you should confer with your advisor to interpret and reaffirm the committee's decisions and recommendations. This is the time to compare notes and get a complete understanding of what transpired at the meeting. It is especially important if substantive changes are required. At this time, you should review your timeline with your advisor and discuss any changes based on the outcomes of the proposal meeting. This is a good time to work with your advisor to revise your dissertation completion schedule and Gantt chart (see Chapter 6 for examples).

SUMMARY

Holding the proposal meeting represents a vital step in the dissertation process. At this meeting, you and your committee discuss your proposed study relative to its scope, design, instrumentation, and significance. You also agree on expectations and procedures for the study's duration.

You are now ready to make final preparations for the peak. This involves analyzing and presenting the results of your study. The next chapter guides you in understanding the data and presenting your findings.

RESOURCES

Doodle

- https://doodle.com/en/

Google Calendar Appointment Slots

- https://support.google.com/calendar/answer/190998?hl=en

National Conference of State Legislators, Tips for Making Effective PowerPoint Presentations

- https://www.ncsl.org/legislators-staff/legislative-staff/legislative-staff-coordinating-committee/tips-for-making-effective-powerpoint-presentations.aspx

PART IV

Final Preparations for the Peak

Source: https://istockphoto.com/hadynyah

May your dreams be larger than mountains and may you have the courage to scale their summits.

—Harley King

Presenting the Findings

12

You have gathered your interview, survey, test, archival, and/or observation data and are ready to make additional headway up the mountain—analyzing and presenting the findings of your study. Specific data analysis techniques are beyond the scope of this book; the resources section at the end of this chapter is intended to help you through your analytical trek.

The purpose of this chapter is to report the findings of your study as clearly and succinctly as possible. Usually, you present findings in a narrative format supplemented by tables or figures. Tables display numerical data in rows and columns, whereas figures include any illustration other than a table (e.g., graphs, charts, diagrams, photographs, etc.).

As a general rule, the findings from your study should be presented objectively and without editorializing or speculating—free from author bias. Occasionally, data interpretation is merged with the findings. Consult with your dissertation advisor to ascertain his or her preference regarding this issue.

Understanding the Data

Understanding the Data in a Quantitative Study

Carefully review the data prior to creating tables or writing the narrative. Using your highlighting tool on the computer, color-code the data. Use a different color for each research question and highlight those data directly related to each research question. This will assist you in finding the information for each of your research questions.

Know what the statistics mean, which are relevant, and which are unimportant. Go over every aspect of your data, research question by research question. If you're paying a statistician for his or her expertise, arrange for interpretation to be part of the services.

Understanding the Data in a Qualitative Study

If you are analyzing qualitative data (e.g., narratives, such as interview transcripts; visuals, such as art or videos; audio, such as recordings; or observations and artifacts), take the time to become thoroughly familiar with your data, to make sense of what people said and to integrate the different responses.

Conducting an analysis of qualitative data requires that you review and read through all your data from beginning to end several times. Only then can you realistically generate categories, themes, and patterns that emerge from the data. A description of one coding process for developing themes and patterns is provided in Chapter 10. Similarly, observation data and analysis of artifacts should be analyzed for emergent themes and patterns.

Writing the Introductory Paragraph

Begin this chapter with an introductory paragraph. Open with a sentence that briefly describes the problem and then explain the chapter's organization. Glatthorn and Joyner (2005) provided an illustration of what you might write:

> As stated in Chapter 1, the study reported here examined in detail the problems encountered by teachers as they developed and used performance assessments in their planning and teaching. The chapter is organized in terms of the two specific research questions posed in Chapter 1. It first reports the problems they encountered in developing performance assessments; it then examines the difficulties they experienced in using those assessments in their teaching. (p. 200)

The introductory paragraph is often followed by a demographic description of the participants (gender, age, experience, etc.). These may be written or presented in a graphic format such as a chart or table.

Tables and the Narrative Description

Now it is time to create your tables and the accompanying narrative to tell the story of your findings. How well the tables and narrative support each other affects the quality of your communication. It is important that your tables, figures, and graphics are clear, concise, and easy to read. Also, remember to locate tables, figures, and graphics as closely as possible to the text that discusses them.

HELPFUL HINT

Be sure to consult your advisor about her or his preferences on the interaction between the graphics and the narrative. Some advisors believe the tables or other graphics should stand alone and the narrative should stand alone; that is, the narrative should state exactly what is in the tables/graphics. Others prefer that the narrative highlight what is in the tables/graphics, which means the reader grasps the full meaning only when the tables/graphics are read.

Plan Before You Write

The first question to ask yourself is this: *Should my data be reported as a table, graph, diagram, chart, and so on, or should they simply be described in writing?* One helpful approach in planning this chapter is to create all your tables, figures, and graphics before you do any actual writing. This makes the writing task much easier. Plus, taking time to arrange and report your data in different forms and in different ways (tables, etc.) stimulates your thinking and helps you to discover surprises or trends you might have overlooked. The information contained in these tables/graphics helps you clarify the data and provides the basis for writing the narrative.

Presenting the Findings

Your presentation of findings depends on the nature of your research. A variety of organizational strategies are available. For example, you can organize your data chronologically, by variable, by hypothesis, by research question, by theme and pattern, or by any other approach appropriate for your study.

Organizing your data by research question is a good way to clearly discuss your findings and to maintain consistency among chapters. The research questions drive headings—not necessarily the research question itself but rather a heading that describes the question. Then, under each heading, present the findings related to that question, including the narrative and the various statistical analyses.

Qualitative Data

Qualitative data are usually presented in narrative form. Information is organized into themes, categories, or patterns. Often accompanying the narrative are tables, figures, or graphics that complement and simplify large amounts of information.

Qualitative analysis is an emerging process and requires thoughtful judgments about what is significant and meaningful in the data. Confer with your advisor about how to best present the rich data that flow from qualitative procedures. The resource section in this chapter offers materials that can assist you in presenting qualitative data.

HELPFUL HINT

After writing the findings from your first research question (first case, first hypothesis, and so on), send it to your advisor for approval. Obtaining approval of the style and format at this early stage saves you endless hours of rewriting. Plan on creating multiple drafts (even if you were class valedictorian). It's always a good practice to ask a knowledgeable researcher who is objective to read this chapter before sending it to your advisor. Clarity and precision are essential, and objective readers provide valuable assistance.

Guidelines for Designing Tables and Figures

Specific guidelines are required in developing and presenting graphic information. Carefully review your editorial style manual for detailed information and examples of the method and format for each kind of graphic. The following are some suggestions for creating effective graphics:

- Write table titles that report exactly what is in the table.
- Label every column and every row.

- Avoid using too many numbers.

- Report group sizes (and avoid reporting percentages for small groups).

- Keep percentages to tenths (in many instances, whole numbers will suffice).

- Check with your dissertation advisor and university guidelines for direction.

HELPFUL HINT

Tables, graphs, and other graphics should offer ample information that is clear and concise and provide support for the study. Show your graphics to others to get a sense of their understanding.

Concluding Paragraph

Write a paragraph that summarizes all of your key findings and explains what you discovered. Then direct the reader to the following chapter.

Questions to Ask About the Presentation of Findings

1. Are the findings clearly presented?

2. Are the tables, figures, and other graphics well organized and easy to understand?

3. Does each table and/or graphic stand on its own without narrative explanation?

4. Do the tables and/or graphics use the format specified by your required style manual and your university?

5. Are the important or notable data in each graphic described in the text?

6. Are the graphics and narrative effectively integrated without unnecessary repetition?

7. Are the findings reported accurately and objectively?

8. Is factual information separate from interpretation and evaluation?

9. Are the data organized by research question?

10. Is there a summary of the key findings at the end of the chapter?

SUMMARY

This chapter presented some recommendations for analyzing and presenting the findings of your study. General guidelines were presented for writing the introductory paragraph and designing and presenting tables and graphics with accompanying narrative. The chapter concluded with some questions to ask yourself about presenting findings and technical references.

RESOURCES

APA Style Blog

- https://apastyle.apa.org/blog/

Minitab, Analyzing Qualitative Data, Part 1: Pareto, Pie, and Stacked Bar Charts

- https://blog.minitab.com/en/applying-statistics-in-quality-projects/analyzing-qualitative-data-part-1-pareto-pie-and-stacked-bar-charts

Oxbridge Essays

- https://www.oxbridgeessays.com/

Statistics By Jim, "Guide to Data Types and How to Graph Them in Statistics" by Jim Frost

- https://statisticsbyjim.com/basics/data-types/

Scribbr, "How to Write a Results Section: Tips & Examples" by Tegan George

- https://www.scribbr.com/dissertation/results/

Conclusion and Recommendations 13

Great is the art of beginning, but greater is the art of ending.

—Henry Wadsworth Longfellow

It is time to write the last chapter and begin the final ascent on the dissertation journey. This entails explaining to your readers what your findings mean, providing a brief summary of the entire study, and presenting conclusions and recommendations about the topic.

Since this chapter is written at the very end of the dissertation process, it may seem anticlimactic; however, in many ways, it is the dissertation's apex chapter. It provides meaning to the problem stated in the introductory chapter and offers answers to the research questions or hypotheses/null hypotheses in the methods chapter. This chapter is likely to be the one that researchers will read first, as readers typically turn to this chapter to get a whole sense of the research and the implications for the discipline. In other words, it is the sine qua non.

Reflect on Findings

Before beginning to write this chapter, take time to reflect on the findings and implications of your study. Don't rush this most important phase. For the reader, this is the most interesting aspect of your dissertation. Spend time away from your research so that when you return to it, you can put it in perspective and gain deeper insights.

This is the point in the process where you shift from being a reporter to becoming an informed and knowledgeable authority. You are the one closest to the focus of your study, its progress, and its data. You now have the responsibility to tell others about what your findings mean and to integrate your findings with current theory, research, and practice. Considerable thought and diligent reflection are required when interpreting research findings.

HELPFUL HINT

One way to reflect on your study prior to writing this chapter is to imagine giving a five-minute presentation to a scholarly group or to a professional organization. In a few sentences, summarize what your study means. What three main conclusions would you share with the group? How would you frame the study so that others can understand it? How might you take theory to practice in clarifying the relevance of the findings and generating audience interest? What new questions are sparked by your findings?

Chapter Organization

This chapter will vary, depending on your research methods, your findings, and the guidance of your advisor and your university's guidelines. There is no one way to organize this chapter. Consider discussing the meaning of your study using creative alternatives that add interest for the reader. Some qualitative researchers generate interest through scenarios, letters, and dialogues. Quantitative researchers are likely to use graphs, tables, and various other graphics to assist the reader in visualizing the findings. A traditional "Conclusions and Recommendations" chapter usually includes any combination of the following elements:

- Introduction
- Summary of the study
  - Overview of the problem
    - Purpose statement
    - Research questions and/or hypotheses and null hypotheses
    - Summation of the methodology
    - Overview of the sample, data collection, and analysis
    - Synopsis of major findings

- Findings related to the literature
- Unanticipated findings
- Conclusions
  - Implications (discipline-specific) for scholars
  - Implications for the profession
  - Implications for the field
  - Recommendations for further research
  - Concluding remarks

Introduction

Write a brief introductory paragraph that assists the reader in focusing on the chapter's organization and content. Here is an example:

> This chapter presents a summary of the study and important conclusions drawn from the data gathered, analyzed, and presented throughout the study. It provides a discussion of the discipline-specific effects and includes implications for the profession. The chapter concludes with recommendations for further research.

Summary of the Study

This section contains the summary of your study—a mini version of all previous chapters. It should stand alone as a description of your study and be sufficient in detail, without undue repetition, so the reader can grasp the entire study without referring to previous chapters.

Your summary should include a brief overview of the problem, the purpose statement, research questions and/or hypotheses and null hypotheses, a review of the methodology, and a summary of the major findings. In the methodology review, it is appropriate to include an overview of the type of research, data collection procedures, and data analysis techniques.

Findings Related to the Literature

Relating your findings to the literature may be contained in the major findings section or in the conclusions section, or it may be emphasized as a separate section with its own heading. Wherever you decide to place this section, you are expected to describe the relationship of your study to the literature and to prior research. What are the differences between your study and previous studies? How do your findings compare with those in the literature? How do they fit or not fit into the findings of previous studies? Do your findings help clarify contradictions in the literature? Do your findings have any special importance, either as improvements over prior findings or in breaking new ground?

Your study may have implications for current theory. You may have found evidence that supports or negates existing theory. If so, point this out. It is important to clearly state the ways your study contributes to the current knowledge base specific to the discipline.

Unanticipated Findings

Unanticipated findings are the surprises that are unexpected outcomes of your study. What uncontrolled variables or circumstances may have influenced the results? Unanticipated findings could occur within your sample, with the instrumentation used, in the responses from participants, in test results, and so on. Be sure to provide the reader with your analysis of the unusual results and/or challenges or surprising outcomes. You may choose to include this information in various sections or create a separate section to discuss these findings. Your dissertation advisor can guide you in structuring any unanticipated findings.

Conclusions

Conclusions represent the result of careful thinking based on evidence supported by research. This is your chance to have the last word on the subject. Writing conclusions well relies on your ability to be a critical and creative thinker—to analyze, synthesize, and evaluate information. Drawing conclusions from findings drives you to go deeper and consider broader issues, make new connections, and expand on the significance of your findings. With the support of the literature and findings, you are granted some leeway to express your own voice and assist the reader in making sense of your findings. However, you are required to make plausible explanations, speculate, and draw conclusions warranted by your findings. In research, your conclusions cannot be subjective opinions.

Your problem statement and literature review were organized to lead the reader from a broad general view of the topic area to specific issues that became the focal point of your study. In this section, you can reverse that approach and lead the reader from the particular findings of your study and introduce generalized interpretations of those findings.

HELPFUL HINT

When discussing or explaining findings, be careful about choosing your words. Use qualifiers such as *seems, appears, possible, probably, likely,* or *unlikely* when addressing causality, suggesting explanations, generalizing to a larger population, or identifying reasons why certain events occurred in the study.

REMEMBER

1. One conclusion may cut across more than one finding.

2. It is important that you don't confuse *findings* and *conclusions*. *Findings* are "the facts," whereas *conclusions* represent a higher level of abstraction—going beyond mere facts to higher levels of interpretation, analysis, and synthesis of findings. Try not to restate the research findings differently.

3. All conclusions must be backed up by your data and/or supported by the literature.

4. Don't add anything in this section not previously presented in the findings chapter.

5. Try not to use hyperbolic language, such as "The results of this study are essential." If done carefully and properly, your study will stand on its own merit.

Implications for Scholars and Professionals

Your research findings have implications that are discipline-specific for other scholars. This is one of the areas where a thorough review of the literature reflects your expertise in the subject and affords you the opportunity to indicate how the findings of your study add to the body of literature on the subject.

It is more than likely that your findings have research and practical implications that will be of interest to the field. In Chapter 1, you included a section titled "Significance of the Study." While preparing for this significance section, you considered who will likely benefit from your study, what they will learn from it, and how they will gain from this knowledge. The section from Chapter 1 now becomes the basis for preparing your implications. In other words, describe how the findings of your study affect future research and practice. Remember that the actions you recommend must be based on your findings, not on opinions.

Recommendations for Further Research

You are expected to present recommendations for ways the topic and findings of your study can be advanced and might contribute to the field. In addition, this is the bridge to suggesting how researchers might take these findings further. These recommendations may arise from constraints imposed on your study, such as conditions you could not or chose not to control. The recommendations can also stem from the study limitations. Some examples of limitations include population and sample, study size, methodology, environment, geography, policy, and when the study was conducted.

Concluding Remarks

Include a summary statement that pulls together your comments and highlights the main points of the chapter. If your dissertation advisor deems it appropriate, this is also a suitable place to include some insights or inspirations derived from conducting your study.

Questions for Summarizing and Discussing the Conclusions:

1. Is there a brief summary of the problem, the methodology, and the findings?

2. Are the findings and conclusions clearly stated?

3. Are the conclusions derived from the findings?

4. Are the conclusions discussed within the framework of previous studies, theory, and the literature base?

5. Are generalizations confined to the population from which the sample was drawn?

6. Are the implications justified by the data?

7. Are recommendations for future research made?

SUMMARY

Chapter 5 of your dissertation summarizes the entire dissertation and interprets the findings. Readers frequently turn to this chapter first to obtain a broad picture of your research. For that reason, suggestions on the content and organization of this final chapter were provided, along with tips and a list of questions to help you reflect on what to include.

Now for the final ascent! You have the opportunity to defend your study. The next chapter offers guidelines about the defense meeting.

Finis! **Congratulate yourself and celebrate writing your last paragraph!**

RESOURCES

American Psychological Association, "Discussing Your Findings" by Beth Azar

- https://www.apa.org/gradpsych/2006/01/findings

Scribbr, "How to Write a Thesis or Dissertation Conclusion" by Tegan George and Shona McCombes

- https://www.scribbr.com/dissertation/write-conclusion/

View from the Summit and Beyond

Live your life each day as you would climb a mountain. An occasional glance toward the summit keeps the goal in mind. . . . Climb slowly, steadily, enjoying each passing moment, and the view from the summit will serve as a fitting climax for the journey.

—Harold V. Melchert

The Final Defense 14

It usually takes more than three weeks to prepare a good impromptu speech.

—Mark Twain

The final defense of your dissertation is the culmination of your doctoral journey. You have worked long and hard and have hopefully produced a scholarly piece of work of which you can be proud. Your advisor and committee members also take pride and pleasure in your accomplishment.

This chapter was written to guide your thinking as you prepare for the final defense. It explains the final defense process by describing a typical defense scenario, the roles of the participants, and the potential outcome criteria.

The doctoral final defense provides the opportunity to speak publicly about your research and is a long-standing tradition in academia. Its major purpose is to demonstrate your ability to advocate for and justify your study, including your research problem, research questions, methodology, findings, and conclusions. In most instances, it is an exciting, collegial experience. Those present at the defense vary from one institution to another, but generally they include your advisor, other committee members, other interested academic community members, colleagues, family, and friends.

Your final defense is scheduled only when you, your advisor, and the committee are satisfied that your work is substantially complete and reflects the standards of high-quality research. Remember, not only is your reputation on the line but also that of your advisor, who has been the principal guide and evaluator of your work. It is important that you present to committee members the best possible final draft of your dissertation—one that has been carefully edited to reduce errors. Allow at least two to four weeks for committee members to review the final copy of your dissertation.

In collaboration with your dissertation chair and committee, arrange for the date, time, and place of the defense. The defense date should allow sufficient time for the required procedures and approvals (check with your university for processes).

Virtual Participation Options

Some universities permit committee members and others to participate in the final defense remotely. With advances in technology, many universities provide remote options for the final defense of the dissertation. Such options might include using software such as Zoom, Skype, Adobe, Google, Facetime, and so on. If this option is available, it is important to plan for the logistics, including technology needs and scheduling.

Logistics for Virtual Defense Participation

- Be aware of different time zones when scheduling the defense. Participants will need access to technology (e.g., computer, webcam).

- Distribute any materials in advance to the committee and participants so they can view these materials on their own computer or mobile device during the presentation.

- Ensure that remote participants are able to see and hear the presentation being made. Try to remove all distracting noise from your environment. A barking dog, crying baby, and so on in the background diverts your audience's attention.

- Consider having a backup system in which the remote participants can interact with the proceedings.

- Plan ahead for such things as dropped calls and disruptions in technology and for completing forms, including obtaining necessary signatures.

A Defense Scenario

What does a final defense look like? Although the format and roles may vary from institution to institution and from advisor to advisor, most follow some common procedures. Here is a scenario that represents a typical final defense.

1. Arrive (log on) early to make sure that the system is working properly. Be considerate of your committee and guests.
   Your advisor moderates the meeting, usually opening with introductions. The advisor introduces the committee members and guests. You then introduce any family or friends who are present.

2. Your advisor explains the purpose of the final defense and the procedures to be followed in conducting the defense.

3. You may be asked to provide a brief overview of your study. If this occurs, the overview may include the following:
   a. The purpose of your study and the research questions
   b. The literature that supports and disagrees with your study
   c. The methods used and reasons for selection
   d. Major findings and conclusions from the findings
   e. Implications of the findings for the scholarly field, for professional applications, and other areas such as policy
   f. Recommendations you would make for further research
   g. It's a good idea to present this summary with minimal notes. It's important that you discuss the overview and the entire process with your advisor/chair prior to the defense.

4. Who asks the first question is a matter of advisor preference. Members of the committee ask their questions either randomly or systematically.

5. When committee members have finished with their questions, your advisor may invite visitors to ask questions or provide comments.

6. Each university and advisor has certain processes that are followed. One such process may include asking you and your guests to allow time for the committee to deliberate and decide on the outcome of your defense. Once the committee has deliberated, the advisor can then invite you to rejoin the committee.

7. Although these decisions vary from institution to institution, ultimately, the committee decides among the following options:

    a. Pass with no revisions

    b. Pass with minor revisions

    c. Pass with major revisions

    d. Defense to be continued

    e. Fail

    What is the difference between minor and major revisions? Minor revisions are those changes that require less substantial rewriting. Possible examples include literature additions, correcting tables, adding more conclusions or recommendations, and editing. Most minor revisions can be completed in a reasonable amount of time.

    Major revisions involve a substantial rewrite of particular sections. Major errors may include incorrect statistics, inconsistency between the research questions and findings, an incomplete literature review, or a lack of adequate data.

8. If you pass or pass with modifications, you receive hearty congratulations by all. You will remember the happy moment when your advisor and committee members congratulate you.

9. At the appropriate time, discuss the revisions with your advisor and clarify procedures for final approval and sign-off.

REMEMBER

Most universities do not permit you to officially use the title of "Doctor" in your professional life until you have completely finalized the dissertation process and the doctorate is administratively posted.

Prior to the Final Defense

The following are some things for you to consider in the days prior to, during, and after the final defense:

- Read your dissertation carefully so you can respond readily and confidently to the questions asked. Play devil's advocate with yourself and try to identify as many of your study's weaknesses as possible.

- Gather a few of your doctoral peers to pose questions so that you can practice potential answers.

- Make sure you are familiar with the most recent work published. The more familiar you are with the relevant literature on your topic, the more knowledgeable you will appear about your field.

- Be prepared to discuss how your findings relate to the literature—both theoretical and practical.

- Try to anticipate what committee members will ask you. List the things you know you will be asked and practice your responses. Also, list questions you wouldn't like to be asked and practice answering them.

- Prepare for questions about why you chose one method rather than another or one statistical procedure over another. Be sure you thoroughly understand any statistics used in your study. Even if you consulted a statistician for assistance in analyzing the numbers and subsequent interpretation, you are the person who is responsible for explaining your rationale and use of the selected statistical procedures.

- Here are some additional questions you might think about:
  - What were the surprises for you?
  - What brought you to explore this particular topic?
  - What were your key learnings about research?
  - What does your study offer to professionals in your field?
  - What are the strengths and weaknesses of your study?
  - Were you to start over, what would you do differently?
  - What was the most significant aspect of the work you've done?
  - Since you wrote your literature review, have you noticed any new work that has been published?
  - How will you communicate your work to other scholars in your field?
  - What did you learn about your subject area? About yourself?

Additional Reflections Prior to the Defense:

- Do some deep reflections on the value of your dissertation to the scholarly field. Who are the people and groups that might profit from your findings? What recommendations would you make to these people?

- Use the few weeks before your final defense to continue contemplating your study. As you do this, you will have fresh insights and new "ah-has" from time to time. Write them down and bring them to your final defense to share with the committee.

- Look for errors—you will always find them—either typographical or in the data. Note what they are and bring a list to the defense. Your committee will appreciate your efforts to produce high-quality work.

- Talk to recent graduates and ask about their experiences and the questions they were asked.

- Attend other final defenses, especially those conducted by your advisor. Seeing the final defense in action relieves the mystery and angst surrounding it.

- Conduct a mock defense in which a group of your colleagues simulate a final defense by acting as your committee. You will probably find their questions more difficult than those posed by the real committee. Be sure to build in time for feedback on your performance.

- Prepare a brief overview of your dissertation and practice presenting it without notes.

- Practice. Practice. Practice.

- Get a good night's sleep and visualize your ideal final defense.

During the Final Defense

- Breathe deeply and stay calm! You want to appear relaxed and confident.

- Maintain eye contact while you are listening to and answering questions. Remember to smile occasionally. It has a positive effect on your committee and improves your mindset.

- With your advisor's permission, you may be able to use notes and/or consult your dissertation; tabs for important sections may be helpful. Trust yourself. You are more knowledgeable than anyone about your topic.

- Really listen to the questions. Don't jump to the conclusion that you know where the person is going and cut him or her off. Let the committee member state the entire question.

- Be appreciative of any criticisms and suggestions to improve your study. Acknowledge the person's contribution and accept it with humility, grace, and gratitude; it is a gift.

- Expect to be asked questions that are not completely clear. When a question is posed that you do not completely understand, ask that the question be rephrased or restated.

- Create some think time for yourself by pausing before responding and/or paraphrasing the question before answering.

- Try to formulate sharp, precise answers. It is better to answer the question first and then elaborate more if needed. Sometimes a question requires a response that goes beyond the data or findings of your study. It is appropriate to acknowledge that something is beyond your study.

- Take time to collect your thoughts. If you don't know the answer to a question, there is no harm in saying, "I don't know." It is better to tell the truth than to fake it. Remember the proverb, "When you find yourself in a hole, stop digging." The stronger your dissertation, the deeper the committee members may want to explore your findings.

- Feel free to show enthusiasm for your study. After all, you spent tremendous amounts of time and energy in conducting the research and preparing your dissertation.

- Consider having someone take notes for you. The notes should focus on the specific suggestions and changes that each committee member requests. Comments should be labeled with the name of the person who requested the change or made a comment. Your advisor is the final arbitrator of the changes to be made.

- Be sure to thank those in the room who have helped you along this dissertation journey. This includes not only your committee members but also any family members and friends who have supported you in this incredible endeavor.

REMEMBER

Remember these encouraging thoughts:

- You know more about your dissertation than anyone else.

- You are the expert on your topic.

- Your months of concentrated reading and research contributed to a unique knowledge of your topic that few others possess.

- Others want you to succeed. You completed a rigorous piece of research, and you should be proud to discuss it publicly.

- Look forward to being welcomed into the community of scholars!

After the Final Defense

- If your committee asks for revisions, complete them as soon as possible. Don't lose any momentum. Usually, you can incorporate minor revisions in a reasonable amount of time. Major revisions take longer, depending on the issues involved. Be very clear about what needs to be altered. Find out the university's protocol for completion of the dissertation processes.

- Celebrate this exhilarating experience with friends, colleagues, and loved ones. By all means, take pictures to record this memorable event.

SUMMARY

The final defense of your dissertation represents the culmination of your doctoral journey. It provides the opportunity to speak publicly about your research and to defend it. This chapter provided an overview of the process and some helpful hints to prepare for events prior to, during, and after the final defense. It can be an exhilarating experience for you, your committee, friends, and family. Commencement follows—that special time when you stand on top of the mountain.

Like all mountain climbers, however, you must eventually descend. The next chapter discusses the experience and ways you can mentor others as they attempt the same journey. This final chapter, titled "Future Peaks," helps you think about ways to disseminate your study's findings to the knowledge base in your field.

RESOURCES

Columbia University, Hints for PhD Defenses

- https://www.cs.columbia.edu/~hgs/etc/defense-hints.html

VirtualSpeech

- https://virtualspeech.com/

Enago Academy, "13 Tips to Prepare for Your PhD Dissertation Defense" by Shrutika Sirisilla

- https://www.enago.com/academy/tips-prepare-phd-dissertation-defense/

Toastmasters International

- https://www.toastmasters.org/

Future Peaks 15

Each fresh peak ascended teaches something.

—Sir Martin Convay

Congratulations! You have successfully completed and defended your dissertation. You now know what it is like to stand on top of a high mountain. The view is amazing, and the exhilaration and pride of achievement unforgettable. It's a peak experience. This is the time for celebration, picture taking, and rejoicing with family, friends, and colleagues. All those who supported you through this long, arduous journey can now revel in your accomplishments and share with you the grandeur of commencement. Rejoice in commencement! It is a mountaintop experience worthy of celebration.

The joyous experience of commencement, with all the various activities associated with it, will be remembered as one of your life's momentous occasions. Like all climbs, though, you must descend. The descent causes some to experience a sense that something is missing. These are normal feelings caused by intense concentration in completing your coursework and dissertation over a prolonged period of time. During this time, you return to a normal life and reacquaint yourself with family and friends.

The Descent

As all climbers must eventually descend the mountain and return to the valley floor, so too must newly minted doctors return to normal life activities and reflect on future scholarly and/or professional opportunities. Experienced mountaineers know that the descent can be difficult and rife with new challenges. Doctoral students often report mixed feelings about completing their study. There is a sense of accomplishment mixed with change, such as parting with friends with whom they bonded and finishing the doctoral program.

This emotional letdown is quite normal, given the pressure of trying to juggle one's personal and professional lives for several years. The dissertation is an overpowering presence that consumes much of your attention. Even though there is a sense of relief in having it over, for most, there is also a sense of loss. Making the transition to a life sans the doctoral marathon may take a while as you deal with the myriad of feelings associated with establishing a routine.

After the dissertation, you have all these extra hours. Take some time to regain your energy and indulge yourself in pleasurable pastimes so often sacrificed—hobbies, books, movies, vacations, regular workouts, and so on. Certainly, it is a good idea to reacquaint yourself with family and friends who are, no doubt, anticipating your return.

Not only is it desirable to rebalance your personal life, but refocusing your professional agenda keeps your career moving ahead. After all, you probably decided to earn the doctorate for a number of reasons, including to advance your career goals. You've invested years and money toward this worthwhile endeavor. In the process, you completed a research study that added a new piece to the scholarly field and offers an opportunity for others to learn from your research.

Taking It Forward

The final dissertation chapter usually contains a section titled "Implications" in which the author makes actionable suggestions to the field directly related to the study's findings. Frequently, recommendations are made to advance the findings, such as taking theory to practice through new innovations, training programs, handbooks, manuals, and media such as websites or videos. Taking the time to follow up on creating these products makes a practical and greatly appreciated contribution to the field.

Disseminate Your Study's Findings

How better to help others than to contribute your study's findings to the knowledge base in your discipline? Every study builds on previous studies. If yours is not available to others, it can't be used to extend knowledge. Remember, you are now an authority on your subject, and as a person with an earned doctorate, you are expected to take your findings forward to inform the field.

It is natural to want to avoid it after working on it so hard and so long. However, letting it sit on the shelf for a long period of time risks not taking it to the next step: sharing your results with a wider audience. It also keeps you from taking full advantage of the professional opportunities it may afford you. Instead of ignoring it, take some time that you devoted each week to writing the dissertation and work on ways to disseminate your research and extend your scholarly and professional network. Presenting your study, publishing, and creating products are ways to disseminate your research. Making your research available to a wider audience beyond your committee opens up a wide array of opportunities and is one of the best ways to contribute knowledge to your field and advance your career.

> A life lived for others is the only one worth living.
>
> —Albert Einstein

Presenting Your Research

A good first step is to present your research to scholarly and/or professional associations in your field and obtain feedback from the participants. Presentations can be made at regional, state, national, and international conferences. Conveners are always on the lookout for presenters and are quite receptive to new and interesting findings in their field. Conferences include a variety of formats, such as paper presentations, panel discussions, poster sessions, leading workshops, formal addresses, and innovative formats such as TED Talks. Scholarly conferences may also be convened on-site and/or online. Scan scholarly and professional organizations, websites, and journals for calls for papers and formal invitations to submit a proposal. The proposal guidelines note the mode of presentation and required length of the proposal as well as the requirements. If you decide to pursue presenting your study at conferences, remember that submissions must be sent in by the due date, which is generally many months in advance of the conference.

Preparing and Submitting Your Presentation

- Go to a conference website and take time to research the process.

- Decide on format (e.g., paper, panel, table, poster, virtual, or in person).

- Read the submission guidelines and follow them to the letter.

- Consider how your submission will be reviewed (e.g., peer review, blind review).

- Research your topic, select ideas, support with the literature, *and most importantly,* follow all requirements, guidelines, and conference focus.

- Edit and reedit before submitting.

- Submit by the deadline. (Note that top academic conferences have a hard deadline and don't permit late submissions.)

Publish Your Research

There are a variety of vehicles where you can publish your research, such as journals, a chapter in an edited book, and so on. Many of these are available in varied formats, including online as well as in hard copy form or an audible format.

Journal Article

Your dissertation research could serve as a basis for a journal article; however, it will need to be rewritten to take a juxtaposed or different view, as academic journals require original content.

It is important that you find a journal that publishes articles that align with your research topic and your particular study. Academic journals focus on empirical and/or theoretical research. Visit your university library website and review the journals in your discipline to get a sense about the requirements and type of articles they publish. Also, be aware that journal websites indicate a quality rating and citation frequency. You can refer to independent citation indexes (e.g., the *Social Science Citation Index* and the *Arts and Humanities Citation Index*). Each journal provides information about how to submit manuscripts for consideration.

- Edit and reedit.

- Review your article per the author guidelines of the journal.

- Check your references carefully.

- Make sure the word count meets the requirements.

The Spirit of Discovery

French poet Rene Daumal wrote an allegorical novel titled *Mount Analogue.* The mountain symbolizes a spiritual voyage of discovery, much like *Pilgrim's Progress* by John Bunyan. As the adventurers in the story ascend the mountain, they discover strange, nearly invisible crystals called *paradama*, symbolic of rare and difficult truths found along the spiritual path. Daumal died before completing the novel but left these words about one of the basic laws of Mount Analogue:

> To reach the summit, one must proceed from encampment to encampment. But before setting out for the next refuge, one must prepare those coming after to occupy the place one is leaving. Only after having prepared them, can one go on up. (Daumal, 1986, p. 104)

You will have many more peaks to climb in your career and in your life. In this parable of Mount Analogue, Daumal exhorts us not to forget those who follow in our footsteps. There are many ways in which you can mentor others as they attempt their journey to the top.

Mentoring

There is no greater gift to those who follow in your footsteps than being available to lend a helping hand as they attempt the dissertation journey themselves. One way is to listen and act as a coach for doctoral students. Frequently, there are opportunities to help apply course work to real situations, provide information about the challenges and the rewards of completing a dissertation, and offer encouragement and support along the path.

Mountain Echos

The following useful dissertation considerations are offered by recent doctoral students and graduates.

Selecting a Topic

A conversation with your chair is really beneficial in shaping and refining your dissertation topic and may also provide you with more clarity and confidence regarding your chosen subject. Choose a topic that you are truly interested in researching, as having a passion for it will make the rest of the dissertation process more enjoyable. (Dr. Weina Chen)

Choose a topic that ignites your passion for learning because you will gain a wealth of knowledge as you immerse yourself in the literature. In turn, this knowledge can be a catalyst for future professional and academic endeavors. (Kimberly Love, doctoral student)

> Wherever we go in the mountains, we find more than we seek.
>
> —John Muir

Create an impactful introduction—this is your moment to captivate the reader with a strong opening statement based on the literature that shows your research is meaningful and engaging. A confident first impression based on the research will also set the tone for your presentation. (Stephanie Voss, doctoral candidate)

Align your research passions and interests with your professional goals when selecting a dissertation topic. Look for a meaningful dissertation topic that will impact you and your field of study. (Ryan Weber, doctoral student)

Planning for Prelims

Be familiar with and know every aspect of your proposal; be the expert. Have a list of potential questions that could be asked during the preliminary defense and be prepared to answer them. (Oghenemano Evero, doctoral candidate)

Rehearse your preliminary presentation a few times and time yourself so that you feel confident during the presentation. (Elizabeth Hollerman, doctoral candidate)

Be consistent. I have learned the importance of using specific language when referencing the triangle of topic, purpose, and main research question. Continuity and linking are foundational to a well-formatted dissertation and proposal. (Mikelle Barberi-Weil, doctoral candidate)

Preparing for the Final Defense

Use the slides as your guide. Practice presenting ahead of time—repetition is very helpful and it aids in the learning process. Don't forget to breathe. (Dr. Natasha Milatovich)

Preparing for the final defense: At this point in the scholar's journey, credibility has been established, and a deep understanding of the literature has revealed a question worthy of an answer. The focus should now turn to transforming research findings and conclusions into a clear and engaging story. (Scott Sorensen, doctoral candidate)

Gaining practice and experience by giving a mock presentation of your final defense is extremely useful. You can present to your peers or anyone else who can provide you meaningful feedback. (Stephanie Voss, doctoral candidate)

Mount Analogue

Along the dissertation journey, you gained new knowledge and wisdom, honed some valuable skills, gained confidence in your abilities as a writer and scholar, and made lasting friendships. However, you cannot stay on the summit forever. Mountain climbers will tell you: What is above knows what is below but what is below does not know what is above. In climbing, always take note of difficulties along the way; as you go up, you can observe them. Coming down, you will no longer see them, but you will know they are there if you have observed them well.

One climbs, one sees. One descends, one sees no longer but one has seen. There is an art to conducting oneself in the lower regions by the memory of what one saw higher up. When one can no longer see, one can at least still know (Daumal, 1952, p. 153).

SUMMARY

Celebrate the joyous high achievement of completing your dissertation and earning your doctorate—a mountaintop experience. However, all climbers must eventually descend and return to post-dissertation life. Some experience an emotional letdown with feelings of loss—this is quite normal following such a long, arduous journey. This is the time to regain energy, indulge in pleasurable pastimes, and think ahead. Some suggestions include creating products as follow-ups to your research, such as seeking opportunities to forward your research through publishing, presenting your research at academic conferences, and speaking about your research to various organizations.

Your next peak represents the opportunity to serve others as a mentor and contribute further to the knowledge base in your field.

> Often when you think you're at the end of something, you're at the beginning of something else.
>
> —Mr. Rogers

RESOURCES

American Psychological Association, "The Perfect Poster" by Michael Price

- https://www.apa.org/gradpsych/2011/01/poster

(Continued)

(Continued)

Harzing.com, "Publish or Perish" by Anne-Wil Harzing

- https://harzing.com/resources/publish-or-perish

Tiny Buddha, "How to Create a Balanced Life: 9 Ways to Feel Calm and Grounded" by Jasmin Tanjeloff

- https://tinybuddha.com/blog/9-tips-to-create-a-balanced-life/

Inside Higher Ed, "Transforming a Dissertation Chapter into a Published Article" by Faye Halpern and James Phelan

- https://www.insidehighered.com/advice/2020/08/27/how-adapt-your-dissertation-so-it-works-published-article-opinion

Purdue University Online Writing Lab (OWL), Academic Proposals

- https://owl.purdue.edu/owl/graduate_writing/graduate_writing_genres/graduate_writing_genres_academic_proposals_new.html

Parting Thoughts

This book was intended to offer useful information and inspiration for completing your dissertation. We hope you found the content and suggestions offered in this book useful and valuable on your dissertation journey. We also hope your journey results in one of the most rewarding personal experiences of your life.

We leave you with two thoughts:

Be positive! A positive mental attitude, more than any other factor, will determine whether you complete your dissertation or not. View obstacles as plateaus on the way to the summit and find ways to surmount them. It takes persistence and determination to finish.

Don't give up! No matter the obstacles you encounter, try to shift gears and keep going. Nothing great comes without effort.

> Real change, enduring change, happens one step at a time.
>
> —Ruth Bader Ginsburg

Tomorrow is not a day of the week. Develop a sense of urgency about completing your dissertation.

> It is not the mountain we conquer, but ourselves.
>
> —Sir Edmund Hillary

Keep climbing! You've got this!

> —LH & CR

Appendix

Dissertation Content Checklist

Consider the following questions when evaluating the quality and completeness of the dissertation document. Determine whether the questions are appropriate depending on the nature of your study (e.g., qualitative verses quantitative). Items within chapters may vary somewhat, based on the preferences of your dissertation advisor and university dissertation guidelines.

Chapter 1

Statement of the Problem

1.1 Is the background of the problem clearly presented?

1.2 Is adequate background presented for all the variables and/or concepts under study?

1.3 Is adequate information presented for an understanding of the problem?

1.4 Is the problem clearly stated?

1.5 Is there a need to know?

1.6 Is it clear how this study will add to the body of knowledge specific to the field of study?

1.7 Is the theoretical base for the study clear and appropriate?

1.8 Is there an appropriate amount of literature cited?

1.9 Is there a description and an analysis of what has already been done related to the problem?

1.10 Is the relationship of the problem to previous research made clear?

1.11 Is there a logical sequence of exposition that leads directly to the purpose statement?

1.12 Is the writing clear and does it follow a line of logic?

1.13 Does the chapter move from the general to the specific?

Purpose Statement

1.14 Is there a call from other authors in the literature for research to be conducted on the purpose of the study and did you cite it?

1.15 Is the purpose of the study stated clearly and succinctly?

1.16 Is the purpose related to the problem statement?

Research Questions

1.17 Are the research questions well stated?

1.18 If the study is quantitative, is the kind of measurement (description, differences, frequency, or relationship) obvious? If the study is qualitative, are the research questions aligned with the key concepts and/or theory?

Delimitations: The Boundaries of the Study

1.19 Are delimitations well defined?

1.20 Are the author's assumptions made clear?

Significance of the Study: What Does Your Study Add to the Body of Knowledge?

1.21 Is there an explanation of how the study will be useful to the academic discipline, and is relevance addressed (e.g., practice and/or policy)?

Definition of Key Terms: Terms Used in the Study That Do Not Have Commonly Known Meanings

1.22 Are the terms used in the study adequately defined so that their usage is understood?

Summary

1.23 Is there a brief summary at the end of the chapter?

Chapter 2

Review of the Literature

2.1 Is the review of the literature comprehensive (i.e., does it cover the major points of the topic)?

2.2 Is there a balanced coverage of all variables or concepts in the study?

2.3 Is there a blend of classic and contemporary references?

2.4 Are there an adequate number of references cited that demonstrate a thorough review of the existing literature?

2.5 Is the review well organized (e.g., are there clear headings and subheadings that guide the reader)? Does it flow logically?

2.6 Are authors who make the same point combined in citations?

2.7 Does the author critically analyze the literature?

2.8 Is there a summary at the end of each major section as well as at the end of the chapter?

2.9 Is there an organizing principle evident in the review or a storyline (e.g., "Four schools of thought," "Six themes that emerge")?

2.10 Are there too many direct quotations?

2.11 Do the direct quotations detract from the readability of the chapter?

Summary

2.12 Is there a brief summary at the end of the chapter?

Chapter 3

Methodology/Research Design

3.1 Is the type of research methodology (e.g., qualitative, quantitative, or multiple methods) introduced as well as the reasons for selecting it?

3.2 Is the type of research design described fully (case study, descriptive, experimental, etc.)?

3.3 Are the variables and/or concepts clearly described?

3.4 Is the design appropriate for informing the research questions?

Purpose and Research Questions or Hypotheses/Null Hypotheses

3.5 Is the study's purpose and the research questions or hypotheses/null hypotheses stated?

3.6 Is the methodology reported in sufficient detail so that you or another researcher could replicate the study without further information?

Human Subjects Protection

3.7 Is human protection training/certification described?

3.8 Are your university institutional review board (IRB) requirements described for conducting research that involves human subjects?

3.9 Is there a description of how the researcher will protect human subjects?

3.10 Is the IRB process and approval (e.g., IRB approval letter) for the researcher to conduct the study included?

3.11 Is a section on research ethics included (e.g., mitigating researcher bias, etc.)?

Sample and Population

3.12 Will the entire population be studied? Or was a sample selected?

3.13 Is the kind of sampling described adequately (random, cluster sampling, purposive, criterion-based sampling, etc.)?

3.14 If the study is quantitative, is the sample size large enough?

3.15 Are the major characteristics of the sample described adequately?

3.16 Are the procedures and criteria for selecting a sample clearly described?

Instrumentation

3.17 Is a rationale given for the selection of the instruments used?

3.18 Is the instrument described in terms of purpose and content?

3.19 If qualitative, will the instrument (e.g., interview questions) yield responses that will inform the research questions? If quantitative, will the instrument (e.g., survey) be appropriate for measuring the variables?

3.20 If an instrument was developed specifically for the study, are the procedures involved in its development described?

3.21 If qualitative, are the processes for establishing credibility, dependability, and trustworthiness described?

3.22 If quantitative, are validity and reliability processes described?

Data Collection

3.23 Are procedures for collecting data described in sufficient detail to permit them to be replicated by another researcher?

3.24 Is a pilot test (or beta test or field test) conducted and described?

3.25 Are the following data collection procedures described: statement of how and when data will be collected, follow-up procedures, and timeline?

Data Analysis and Data Display

3.26 Is there an adequate description of the data analysis processes?

3.27 For qualitative research, are the coding methods described?

3.28 For quantitative research, are the statistical tests described?

3.29 How will data be displayed (e.g., text, narratives, graphics, tables, figures, other visuals such as pictures or photographs, etc.)?

Limitations

3.30 Have you described the limitations of the study?

3.31 Are limitations (such as geography, sample size, tests run, limited access to information, etc.) clearly delineated?

Summary

3.32 Is there a brief summary of the chapter?

Chapter 4

Introduction to Findings

4.1 Have you introduced the chapter and restated the purpose and research questions?

Findings and Data Display

4.2 Are the findings presented clearly in relation to the research questions?

4.3 Are narratives and/or tables, figures, and graphics well organized and easy to understand?

4.4 Are the key data in each table and figure explained objectively in the text?

4.5 Within the themes and patterns of a qualitative study, is there a balance of direct quotations and descriptions to support the meaning of the themes and patterns?

Summary

4.6 Is there a brief summary of the chapter?

Chapter 5

Conclusions and Recommendations: Overview of the Study

5.1 Is there a brief introduction and overview of the problem, the purpose, the methodology, and the findings?

Conclusions: Making Meaning for the Readers

5.2 Are conclusions derived from the findings and clearly stated?

5.3 Are conclusions discussed within the framework of previous studies as well as this study?

5.4 Are findings and conclusions supported by the theoretical or conceptual framework used for the study? Are they supported by the literature?

5.5 Are generalizations confined to the study population/sample?

Implications

5.6 Are implications based on the findings and conclusions discussed?

5.7 Are implications related to the scholarly discipline stated, and are they described clearly?

5.8 Are implications related to the practice of professionals in the field described clearly?

5.9 If relevant, are implications related to policy and policy makers included?

Recommendations for Further Study

5.10 Does this section contain recommendations for further research beyond your study, and did you connect it to your research and findings?

5.11 Did your recommendations for further study include selecting a different population or another site and/or suggesting a different method (e.g., if this study was qualitative, possibly a quantitative method could be applied, etc.)?

5.12 Did your recommendations for further study involve aspects that weren't included in your study but would further knowledge related to the topic or field?

Summary

5.13 Is there a brief summary of the chapter?

References

Abascal, J. R., Brucato, D., & Brucato, L. (2001). *Stress mastery: The art of coping gracefully.* Prentice Hall.

Amdur, R. J., & Bankert, E. A. (2002). *Institutional review board: Management and function.* Jones & Bartlett.

American Psychological Association (APA). (2020). *Publication manual of the American Psychological Association* (7th ed.). American Psychological Association.

Boote, D., & Beile, P. (2005). Scholars before researchers: On the centrality of the dissertation literature review in research preparation. *Educational Researcher, 34*(6), 3–15.

Booth, W. C., Colomb, G. G., & Williams, J. M. (1995). *The craft of research.* University of Chicago Press.

Council of Graduate Schools. (1991). *The role and nature of the doctoral dissertation: A policy statement.* https://files.eric.ed.gov/fulltext/ED331422.pdf

Council of Graduate Schools. (2018-2023). *Annual strategic leaders global summit on graduate education.* https://cgsnet.org/data-insights/international-engagement/global-summit-on-graduate-education/

Creswell, J. W. (2002). *Research design: Qualitative, quantitative, and mixed methods approaches* (2nd ed.). SAGE.

Creswell, J. W. (2004). *Educational research: Planning, conducting, and evaluating quantitative and qualitative research* (2nd ed.). Pearson.

Creswell, J. W. (2007). *Educational research: Planning, conducting, and evaluating quantitative and qualitative research* (3rd ed.). Pearson.

Creswell, J. W. (2009). *Research design: Qualitative, quantitative, and mixed methods approaches* (3rd ed.). SAGE.

Creswell, J. W. (2015). *Educational research: Planning, conducting, and evaluating quantitative & qualitative research* (5th ed.). Pearson.

Creswell, J. W., & Poth, C. N. (2018). *Qualitative inquiry and research design: Choosing among five approaches* (4th ed.). SAGE.

Daumal, R. (1952). *Mount analogue.* Overlook.

Daumal, R. (1986). *Mount analogue.* Penguin.

Davis, J. (2015). *Two awesome hours: Science-based strategies to harness your best time and get your most important work done.* HarperOne.

Denzin, N. K., & Lincoln, Y. S. (Eds.). (2011). *The SAGE handbook of qualitative research* (4th ed.). SAGE.

Finlay, B., & Finlay, C. (2011). *Kilimanjaro and beyond.* Dog Ear Publishing, LLC.

Fitzpatrick, J., Secrist, J., & Wright, D. J. (1998). *Secrets for a successful dissertation.* SAGE.

Galvan, J. L. (2006). *Writing literature reviews.* Pyrczak.

Galvan, J. L., & Galvan, M. C. (2017). *Writing literature reviews: A guide for students of behavioral sciences* (7th ed.). Routledge.

Gay, L. R., & Airasian, P. (1996). *Educational research.* Merrill Prentice Hall.

Gay, L. R., & Airasian, P. (2003). *Educational research: Competencies for analysis and applications.* Merrill Prentice Hall.

Gay, L. R., Mills, G., & Peter, A. (2008). *Educational research: Competencies for analysis and applications* (9th ed.). Merrill Prentice Hall.

Geery, L. (1997). *An exploratory study of the ways in which superintendents use their emotional intelligence to address conflict in their organizations* (Publication No. 10124237). [Doctoral dissertation]. University of La Verne, La Verne, CA.

Glatthorn, A. A., & Joyner, R. L. (2005). *Writing the winning thesis or dissertation: A step by step guide* (2nd ed.). SAGE.

Hart, C. (2004). *Doing a literature search: A comprehensive guide for the social sciences.* SAGE.

Hart, C. (2009). *Doing a literature review.* SAGE.

Hibbs, S. (2004). *Consider it done! Ten prescriptions for finishing what you start.* iUniverse.

Hyatt, L. (2023). *Qualitative research consistency review process.* AERA.

Jast, J. (2015). *Laser-sharp focus: A no-fluff guide to improved concentration, maximized productivity and fast-track to success.*

Johnston, B. (2000). *The effects of looping on parent involvement and student attitudes in elementary classrooms* [Unpublished doctoral dissertation]. University of La Verne, La Verne, CA.

Lincoln, Y. S., & Guba, E. (1986). *Naturalistic inquiry.* SAGE.

Madsen, D. (1992). *Successful dissertations and theses.* Jossey-Bass.

Mark, G., Gudith, D., & Klocke, U. (2008). *The cost of interrupted work: More speed and stress.* https://www.ics.uci.edu/~gmark/chi08-mark.pdf

Martin, R. (1980). *Writing and defending a thesis or dissertation in psychology and education.* Charles C Thomas.

Maslow, A. H. (1968). *Toward a psychology of being.* Van Nostrand Reinhold.

Merriam, S. B. (2001). *Qualitative research and case study applications in education.* Jossey-Bass.

Miles, M. B., & Huberman, A. M. (2014). *Qualitative data analysis: A methods sourcebook.* SAGE.

Miller, A. (2009). *Finish your dissertation once and for all: How to overcome psychological barriers, get results and move on with your life.* American Psychological Association.

Miller, J. I., & Taylor, B. J. (1987). *The thesis writer's handbook.* Alcove.

Newport, C. (2016). *Deep work: Rules for focused success in a distracted world.* Grand Central.

Office for Human Research Protections (OHRP). (1979). *The Belmont report.* U.S. Department of Health & Human Services.

Oliver, P. (2008). *The student's guide to research ethics.* Open University Press.

Oxford Academic. (2018). Instructions to authors. *Behavioral Ecology.* https://academic.oup.com/beheco/pages/information_for_authors

Pascarelli, E. (2004). *Dr. Pascarelli's complete guide to repetitive strain injury: What you need to know about RSI and carpal tunnel syndrome.* Wiley.

Patton, M. Q. (2015). *Qualitative research & evaluation methods: Integrating theory and practice* (4th ed.). SAGE.

Rath, T. (2013). *Eat move sleep: How small choices lead to big changes.* Missionday.

Remenyi, D., Williams, B., Money, A., & Swartz, E. (1998). *Doing research in business and management: An introduction to process and method.* SAGE.

Ridley, D. (2012). *The literature review: A step-by-step guide for students.* SAGE.

Roig, M. (2006). *Avoiding plagiarism, self-plagiarism, and other questionable writing practices: A guide to ethical writing.* https://ori.hhs.gov/avoiding-plagiarism-self-plagiarism-and-other-questionable-writing-practices-guide-ethical-writing

Rossman, G. B., & Rallis, S. F. (1998). *Learning in the field: An introduction to qualitative research.* SAGE.

Rudestam, K. E., & Newton, R. R. (2007). *Surviving your dissertation: A comprehensive guide to content and process* (3rd ed.). SAGE.

Rudestam, K. E., & Newton, R. R. (2015). *Surviving your dissertation: A comprehensive guide to content and process* (4th ed.). SAGE.

Schuller, R. H. (1980). *The peak to peek principle.* Bantam.

Schultz, B. (2008). *Freshmen adjustment to college at the University of Alaska: A descriptive ex post facto study* [Unpublished doctoral dissertation]. University of La Verne, La Verne, CA.

Sieber, J. (1992). *Planning ethically responsible research: A guide for students and internal review boards.* SAGE.

Silver, C., & Lewins, A. (2014). *Using software in qualitative research: A step by step guide* (2nd ed.). SAGE.

Singh, A. A., & Lukkarila, L. (2017). *Successful academic writing: A complete guide for social and behavioral scientists.* Guilford Press.

Spindle, B. (2006). *A study of Alaska native student persistence and academic success at the University of Alaska Anchorage* [Unpublished doctoral dissertation]. University of La Verne, La Verne, CA.

Springer Nature. (2018). How to write a paper: Writing for a nature journal. *Nature.com.* https://www.nature.com/authors/author_resources/how_write.html

Staindack, S., & Staindack, W. (1988). *Understanding & conducting qualitative research.* Kendall/Hunt.

Sternberg, D. (1981). *How to complete and survive a doctoral dissertation.* St. Martin's Press.

Stone, W. C. (1962). *The success system that never fails.* Prentice Hall.

Strong, W. S. (1998). *The copyright book: A practical guide.* MIT Press.

Strunk, W., & White, E. B. (1979). *The elements of style* (3rd ed.). Macmillan.

Strunk, W., & White, E. B. (2000). *The elements of style* (4th ed.). Allyn & Bacon.

Tashakkori, A., & Teddlie, C. (Eds.). (2003). *Handbook of mixed methods in the social and behavioral sciences.* SAGE.

Tracy, B. (2017). *Eat that frog! 21 great ways to stop procrastinating and get more done in less time* (3rd ed.). Berrett-Koehler.

U.S. Copyright Office. (2009). *Copyright information.* https://www.copyright.gov/title17/

U.S. Department of Health and Human Services. (2010). *Code of federal regulations 45 CFR 46, 46.116(a).* https://www.hhs.gov/ohrp/regulations-and-policy/regulations/45-cfr-46/index.html#46.116

Waitley, D. (1987). *Being the best.* Oliver Nelson.

Western Association of Schools and Colleges. (2008). *Handbook of accreditation of the Western Association of Schools and Colleges.* https://wscuc.org

Williams, J. M. (2003). *Style: Ten lessons in clarity and grace* (7th ed.). Addison-Wesley Educational.

Yin, R. K. (2014). *Case study research: Design and methods* (2nd ed). SAGE.

Zinsser, W. (1994). *On writing well: An informal guide to writing nonfiction* (5th ed.). HarperPerennial.

Index

A Sage Company

CORWIN HAS ONE MISSION: to enhance education through intentional professional learning.

We build long-term relationships with our authors, educators, clients, and associations who partner with us to develop and continuously improve the best evidence-based practices that establish and support lifelong learning.